Walther Ziegler

Habermas
in 60 Minutes

My thanks go to Rudolf Aichner for his tireless critical editing; Silke Ruthenberg for the fine graphics; Lydia Pointvogl, Eva Amberger, Christiane Hüttner, and Dr. Martin Engler for their excellent work as manuscript readers and sub-editors; Prof. Guntram Knapp, who first inspired me with enthusiasm for philosophy; and Angela Schumitz, who handled in the most professional manner, as chief editorial reader, the production of both the German and the English editions of this series of books.

My special thanks go to my translator

Dr Alexander Reynolds.

Himself a philosopher, he not only translated the original German text into English with great care and precision but also, in passages where this was required in order to ensure clear understanding, supplemented this text with certain formulations adapted specifically to the needs of English-language readers.

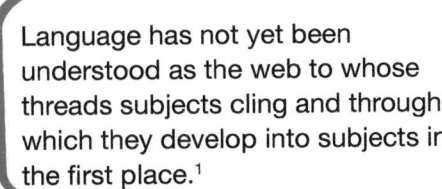

Language has not yet been understood as the web to whose threads subjects cling and through which they develop into subjects in the first place.[1]

Bibliographic Information held by the German National Library: The details of the original German edition of this publication are held by the German National Library as part of the German National Bibliography; detailed bibliographical data can be found online at www.dnb.de.

© 2020 Dr Walther Ziegler
1st Edition October 2020
Jacket design and graphic design for the whole book: Silke Ruthenberg, making use of illustrations by:
Raphael Bräsecke, Creactive – Studio for Advertising, Comics & Illustrations
© JackF - Fotolia.com (image-frames)
© Valerie Potapova - Fotolia.com (image-frames)
© Svetlana Gryankina - Fotolia.com (speech-balloons)

Publisher and Printing:
BoD – Books on Demand, Norderstedt
ISBN 978-3-7526-1237-0

Contents

Habermas's Great Discovery   **7**

Habermas's Central Idea   **24**

The Double Structure of Human Language   24

The Four Validity-Claims and The Stubborn
Wish for Comprehension and Agreement   31

"Am I Driving Here or You?" –
The Four Validity-Claims in Everyday Speech   37

Rationality as the Goal of Every Act of
Linguistic Understanding   49

Domination-Free Discourse and
Discourse Ethics   53

The Development of Humanity Within the
Linguistic Paradigm

Communicative vs. Instrumental Reason   71

Of What Use Is Habermas's Discovery
for Us Today?   **89**

The Struggle Against the Colonization
of the Lifeworld   89

Eugenics, the "Self-Optimization" of
Humanity: Act Communicatively,
Not Instrumentally!   96

The Third Millennium: A New Barbarism or
the Development of Communicative
Rationality?   105
Dare to Engage in Domination-Free
Discourse!   113

Bibliographical References   **129**

Habermas's Great Discovery

Jürgen Habermas (b. 1929) is generally looked on as one of the most important philosophers of the last half of the 20th and first half of the 21st century. His work is known far beyond the borders of Europe. His magnum opus, *The Theory of Communicative Action*, has by now been translated into over forty languages and is the subject of debate worldwide. Habermas has read the works of all the most significant British, American, French and German philosophers, linguists, sociologists, psychologists and psychoanalysts and integrated the ideas of these writers into his own theory. It is, in fact, unlikely that there has ever been another philosopher who succeeded, to the degree that Habermas has, in productively drawing so many key ideas, taken from research done in both present-day and classical philosophy and social science, into his own theory. But what has emerged from this is not, as one might have expected, a mere digest or synopsis of contemporary thought as a whole. No. Despite his massive erudition and the multiplicity of his intellectual interests, Habermas does in the end produce his own highly personal answer to the question of life's sense and meaning.

His great philosophical discovery is both a rousing and a modest one. Rousing because, almost two hundred years after the great philosophers of history Hegel and Marx, Habermas attempts once again to discover a meaning for human history in its entirety, showing that there is reason in this history and that there will continue to be; modest because he describes without any rhetoric or bombast the capacity that humanity has to shape its own future and deduces this capacity, in a highly pragmatic way, from a phenomenon we encounter in our daily life.

Because, whereas for Hegel it was the mystical self-movement of the "World Spirit" that drove history on, and for Marx the drama of "class struggle", Habermas discovers the driving motor of humanity's development rather in a seemingly unremarkable phenomenon that surrounds us all day every day: language.

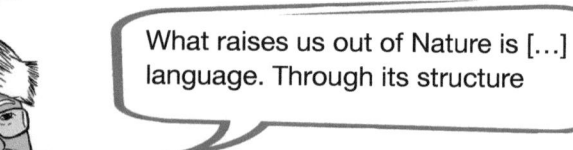

What raises us out of Nature is [...] language. Through its structure

> autonomy and responsibility are posited for us. Our first sentence expresses unequivocally the intention of universal and unconstrained consensus.[2]

In these few brief words we have the core idea, subtle and revolutionary at the same time, of Habermas's philosophy. What "raises us out of Nature", what distinguishes us from plants and animals, is language. All human beings have the capacity for speech. For this reason, Habermas calls language a "species-competence" which belongs, as an innate ability, to human beings already at the moment of our birth and distinguishes us from all other living entities. Communication through language is indeed a faculty which is much more fully formed and developed in human beings than is the case with any other species. In humans it is universal.

Thus, a child that is born in deepest Bavaria but is raised in Beijing will learn to speak Chinese just as perfectly as, conversely, a Chinese child raised in Bavaria will learn to speak German, indeed even the Bavarian dialect of German.

This capacity of human beings to talk with one another is the central starting point for Habermas's philosophy. His discovery of language to be a key phenomenon explaining mind, identity and society has, in fact, a biographical aspect to it that is not without interest. Habermas himself was born with a speech-related handicap, a so-called "hare lip", which, even despite two operations, continued to affect his pronunciation and which often made him, as a child, the butt of other children's mockery. Habermas himself has said that it may well have been this disability that sharpened his attention to the key significance of linguistic communication.

For Habermas, language stands both at the beginning and at the end of humanity's history. It points the way forward for us. And not just a way leading anywhere but a way to a better future. In his famous magnum opus, *The Theory of Communicative Action*, he expounds his great hypothesis regarding development both singular and collective: the learning and the exercise of language leaves profound marks on the development both of the individual and the species and culminates in an insistent claim to the necessity of ever better and ever broader understanding between human beings:

Reaching understanding is the inherent telos of human speech.[3]

"Telos" is the Greek word for "aim" or "goal". The sentence, therefore, means: "reaching understanding is the inherent goal of human speech". But why? Why would language aim in every case at reaching understanding? I can, of course, use language in everyday situations to come to an understanding or agreement with other people. I can use it to arrive at a compromise with others, for example, or even to express solidarity with them and join them in realizing a shared project. But is this enough to prove that mutual understanding is the "telos", or inherent goal, of language? Is Habermas, perhaps, being a little too optimistic here?

Language, one might object here, surely also contains tendencies directly opposite to those evoked by Habermas. I can, after all, equally well use language to curse, insult and otherwise verbally injure other people. It is well-known that words do not always lead to consensus and mutual understanding but rather, on the contrary, very often to conflict and quarrel. Habermas, of course, is aware of these objections to his central thesis. He holds, however, to this radical thesis nonetheless:

Our first sentence expresses unequivocally the intention of universal and unconstrained consensus.[4]

What does Habermas mean by writing that "our first sentence unequivocally expresses" the wish for consensus, that is to say, mutual agreement? This claim has, in the last analysis, a historical dimension. Indeed, it has a prehistoric one. This means nothing other than that our oldest caveman ancestor set, with the very first sentence he spoke to another caveman, a process in motion whose effects reach down to the present day and is still now leading to better and better mutual understanding between human beings. Because whatever this one caveman may actually have said to the other, one thing, says Habermas, lies beyond all question here: the caveman wished that the other should understand what he was saying because, if he had not so wished, he would never have begun to speak at all. And even if the first act of speech in human history had only been a threat or an angry warning, that is to say, an aggressive act, the person performing it surely wished at least to succeed in making the person thus spoken to understand this threat or this warning and tailor his behaviour accordingly.

If, for example, the caveman in question had stood in front of his cave and shouted: "Go away! This hole is mine!" or, as is more probable, had just emitted a loud cry, shaken his fist and shook his club, then even with this language of noises and gestures he had wanted to achieve the result of prompting the other caveman to respect his domicile and move on. In other words, he had wished to come to some sort of understanding with the other and had thereby set a process of mutual understanding in motion, even if it was at the most primitive possible level.

Or perhaps the first words spoken in human history were the warning shouts of a hunter who wanted to alert his fellow tribesman to the presence of a dangerous animal. Or maybe they were gentle hummed words with which a mother put her child to sleep. In all these cases, however, we can say that there began, with the first sentence spoken, an ever-growing exchange of sounds, gestures, words and phrases. Because once the wish for mutual understanding came to be present in the world it inevitably began to exert its peculiarly binding effect, at the end of the development of which Habermas believes there to stand, potentially, a global society in which humanity brings to realization a "universal, uncoerced consensus" of all its members, regardless of their origin, their wealth or their degree of culture. There will then come to rule no longer power or violence but rather, in a phrase of Habermas's that has become very famous, "the unforced force of the better argument"[5].

This highly positive prognosis is, Habermas makes a point of emphasizing, no idealistic assumption but rather a development which can be proven to be firmly anchored in the nature of language itself.

The human interest in autonomy and responsibility is not mere fancy, for it can be apprehended a priori.[6]

And Habermas does in fact succeed, in his magnum opus *The Theory of Communicative Action* and in other works preparatory to this latter, in proving, through a whole series of painstakingly precise micro-analyses, that there is contained in every one of the sentences we speak every day, i.e. in every speech-act of any kind, the seed of a later general mutual understanding, and this quite regardless of when and where these sentences are spoken. For this reason Habermas can confidently write:

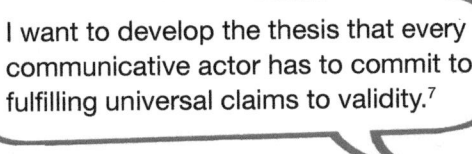

I want to develop the thesis that every communicative actor has to commit to fulfilling universal claims to validity.[7]

Habermas, then, propounds the exciting thesis that every person that speaks automatically raises, whether he wishes to or not, certain "claims". That is to say, he makes certain assumptions and these assumptions must, in the last analysis, tend to result in a rational mutual understanding. Because, Habermas argues, every one of us that ever moves our lips and speaks must in doing so, without stating this explicitly and perhaps without even realizing it immediately, make certain silent assumptions and must also suppose that these assumptions are correct and can be vindicated. These silent assumptions which are implicitly at play in every conversation Habermas calls "universal validity-claims".

One of these "universal validity-claims" consists, for example, simply in the fact that, at the moment at which we start to speak, we make the assumption that the other person can both hear and understand what we are saying. That is to say, that we are speaking loudly enough and that the person spoken to can decipher what we are saying, i.e. that they speak the same national language as us and that they are not, for example, a child who will not yet have mastered the grammatical structures we are using. In short: when we say something, we assume that what is said has a good chance of being heard and understood. Conversely, we assume of our own conversation partner, indeed demand of him, that he too, if he has something to say to me, says it in a manner such that I can understand it.

And this is just a first example of a whole series of such validity-claims implicitly present in language. Habermas's merit is that he has discovered these submerged but nonetheless effective language-internal mechanisms and drawn them up onto the surface.

The sum of these validity-claims, along with their interaction with one another, provide the impulse for an ever-expanding rational mutual understanding. Habermas's great philosophical achievement, then, consists in the deciphering of the implicit effects of language. But that is not all. He also shows us how we can give support to these effects and allow them to develop themselves in ways directed to aims of our own. Right at the beginning of his researches in this direction he wrote:

Language has not yet been understood as the web to whose threads subjects cling and through which they develop into subjects in the first place.[8]

And in his groundbreaking magnum opus *The Theory of Communicative Action* Habermas provided precisely this hitherto-lacking understanding. He explained how language was the key phenomenon on whose "threads" human individuals hang like marionettes. Only through language, indeed, can we recognize ourselves as individuals and as members of the human species and only through language can this species develop in a rational manner. Habermas's thesis, still fascinating today, runs:

> In the validity-claims by which we are obliged, however implicitly, to orient ourselves when we act communicatively there inheres a stubborn, even if constantly suppressed, claim to rationality.[9]

In communicative action, then, i.e. in language, there inheres a "stubborn claim to rationality", even if this latter is constantly suppressed. With this claim Habermas has raised once again, in the rough winds of our modernity, the banner of enlightenment and the demand that social development be guided by reason. Even if human history has been marked by terrible setbacks and definitely irrational decisions, extending even to wars and lapses back into barbarism, there still remains alive, Habermas insists, the rational, humanistic claim that the future must be given a more just and reasonable form. We have no choice in the end, he argues, but to build on reason and rationality:

> I believe that I am able to show that a species that is obliged to use the structures of linguistic communication in order to maintain its physical survival makes itself thereby essentially dependent on reason.[10]

To insist in this way that we are essentially dependent on reason and rationality is also to say, of course, that reason and rationality do exist. And with this latter claim Habermas's philosophy flies directly in the face of the philosophy of his own teachers, Adorno and Horkheimer. These two thinkers had felt able, after two world wars and the Holocaust, to issue only the most blackly pessimistic prognosis regarding humanity's future. Reason, they argued, conceived of as an emancipatory force and associated with the Enlightenment's great call for "liberty, equality and fraternity", had proven an utter failure and was, as a project, at an end. In our modern capitalist word, they went on, reason existed only in the degraded form of "instrumental reason". In other words, the "rational" had become identical with whatever brought profit, power and money; i.e. whatever was "instrumentally" useful. Even the sciences, and quite especially the natural sciences, contended Adorno and Horkheimer, have as their sole concern today such questions as how machines can be more efficiently exploited, how factories, computers and bureaucracies can be optimized, and how individuals can be better trained to be good producers and consumers of products. In this "totally manipulated world", Habermas's own teachers had believed, there was no longer any such thing as objective reason. "Instrumental reason" had taken over completely.

The school of thought, therefore, that was founded by Adorno and Horkheimer, and that came to be known as "Critical Theory" soon settled on a position whereby the philosopher could, and indeed had to, critique this capitalist world and its all-pervading "instrumental reason" but could no longer say from just what objective standpoint such a critique could possibly be conducted. This inasmuch as, on this account, there would no longer be any objective reason by whose standard developments might be measured, since every human being, even philosophers, would be parts of this "totally manipulated world" and thus helpless victims of an instrumental, profit-oriented thinking. This, then, was the terrible conclusion arrived at by Adorno and other of Habermas's mentors: we are all completely manipulated; and only our sense of pain and suffering remains to signal to reason that something in our world is not as it should be.

Habermas certainly accepts that, if he has an intellectual "home" within the various modern philosophical schools, it is surely within this one. He sees himself as a representative of "Critical Theory", since he had been, indeed, at the start of his academic career a teaching assistant of Adorno's and had, at that time, fully shared this latter's critique of the greater and greater encroachment of "instrumental reason" in capitalist society. In Habermas's view, however, his teachers had overlooked one absolutely essential aspect of the whole problem. Besides the "instrumental", capitalist reason that Adorno and Horkheimer showed to have been threatening our "lifeworld" at least since the Enlightenment era on, there has also existed, since time immemorial, "communicative reason", which is capable of pointing out for us an alternative way forward. Because there inheres in language an emancipatory power with the aid of which human beings can resist the excesses of capitalism. Egoism and competing profit-interests may seem to us, above all today, to be powerful forces rooted in human nature; but the fact is that we human beings are capable, with the help of language, of coming to agreements about values and norms which set limits and counterbalances to mere "instrumental reason":

What raises us out of Nature is [...] language. Through its structure autonomy and responsibility are posited for us.[11]

Is it really the case that language "un-forcibly forces" us to act autonomously and responsibly? Does there really inhere in it a certain emancipatory power or is language, in the end, nothing but a neutral instrument, a tool? And if there really is a force inhering in language that promotes the bringing and growing together of humanity in its entirety, then why do we see wars occurring over and over again?

Habermas has answers to all these questions. But

above and beyond this he urges every one of us to make the effort of practicing a "domination-free discourse". Language may indeed contain the seed and also the goal of a worldwide communicative consensus; but the process of arriving at this point is not something that can just be left to automatically occur. It is up to us ourselves. We are able, Habermas argues, to ourselves create the conditions necessary for communicative reason to unfold and develop further. Habermas's most famous philosophical creation, his "discourse ethics", is an excellent instrument given to us to achieve this end.

Habermas's Central Idea

The Double Structure of Human Language

Already before fully working out his ideas about language in his magnum opus Habermas had made, in a study preliminary to this latter, an interesting discovery. Linguistic communication, he argued here, has a complexly shifting dual structure. It unfolds simultaneously on two different levels: the level of content and the level of relation. This second level, he goes on to argue, is one that we tend to overlook, or to perceive only subliminally. But it is always present. Because, as soon as we enter, as speaker or listener, into conversation with another human being, what is at issue is no longer merely the content of what is being said but also how we say it and how we deal with the other person that we are saying it to. In other words, a level of human inter-relatedness is also at play or, as Habermas puts it, a dimension of "intersubjectivity". We pass at the same time automatically onto both these levels:

(a) The level of intersubjectivity, at which the speaker-hearers speak with one another and (b) the level of objects or states of affairs about which they communicate with one another. In every speech act, speakers communicate with one another about objects in the world, about things and events, or about persons and their utterances.[12]

This means that, in every conversation, we are, on the one hand, talking with another person. This can be an old friend, a colleague, our mother, our girl-friend, or a person completely unknown to us whom we may even mistrust. On the other hand, however, we also are talking, in every conversation, about something: about football, politics, the weather or some other topic. We converse, in short, in every case with someone about something, so that every verbal interaction has a "level of content" and a "level of relation".

In most everyday conversations these two levels are

interwoven with one another. And in many such conversations both of them are directly and explicitly expressed. When, for example, a young man calls his girlfriend on the cell phone and says: "I swear that I definitely won't be late this time and will pick you up at the station right on the dot of 6 o'clock. I'll even be there at 10 to 6", he thereby, on the intersubjective "level of relation", gives his girlfriend to understand that she is very important to him, that he loves her so much that he is absolutely determined not to disappoint her this time, as he has in the past, by turning up late. But on the "level of content" he has said no more than that he will be picking her up at the station at 6 o'clock the following day. It is the interplay of these two levels that produces, according to Habermas:

[...] the double structure of the speech act.[13]

This distinction appears at first to be a very trivial one. But in many conversational situations it is of greater consequence than one might think. One simple example illustrates this. We have all had the experience of a conversation "going wrong" even though, on the level of what was actually being said, there was no great point at issue between ourselves and our conversation partner. The reason why this occurs is that the exchange of words on specific topics can be overshadowed by not immediately apparent conflicts on the "relational" level. Our attention, however, is usually directed to the level of topics and conversational "content" alone so that, arguing passionately over details, we find ourselves baffled, in the end, that we have come to no agreement despite the arguments on our side having been good ones.

If, however, later we reflect a little we may recognize very clearly why the conversation "went wrong". We may have offended the other person or may have felt offended ourselves. And if either of the participants in a dialogue, or both of them, feel denigrated on "the level of relation", then the arguments on "the level of content" are usually entirely ineffective, since neither is any longer willing to concede anything to his interlocutor. One may, indeed, go on insistently opposing argument to argument but all this will be in vain as long as the real underlying relational conflict is not alluded to or resolved.

Interestingly, however, as Habermas points out, such experiences of failed communication do not at all lead to resignation. On the contrary: in every new conversation we proceed on the optimistic assumption that agreement will, after all, prove to be possible. Or, in other words, that we will always be able to agree "on the level of content" without problems "on the level of relation" interfering with this. We cherish, that is to say, a conscious or unconscious conviction that we will, if necessary, be able to draw the "relation level" out into the open, make our respective needs explicit, and then continue to discuss "on the content level". This, indeed, is successfully achieved in many conversations. Habermas formulates it in terms of an

[...] ensuring of the possibility that accountable subjects will be capable of withdrawing, at any time, from problematical contexts of interaction and engaging in discourse [...].[14]

"Engaging in discourse" means "stepping out" of any problems or entanglements that might exist at "the level of relation" and continuing to oppose argument to argument, in an unconstrained atmosphere, on the pure "level of content" so as eventually to arrive at an agreement. By "discourse", then, Habermas means something different from everyday communication. With respect to the discovery of truth, "discourse" represents a qualitatively superior level to this latter. A "discourse", then, in contrast to everyday communication, is a conversation which is not, or which is no longer, burdened or distorted by those antipathies that may arise, without the conversation partners' being aware of it, on the "level of relation" and which may be said, therefore, to occur in a purified "ideal speech situation":

The ideal speech situation excludes systematic distortion of communication. Only then is the sole prevailing force the unforced force of the better argument, which

allows assertions to be methodically verified in an expert manner [...].[15]

But this "ideal speech situation", in which the only thing that still counts is "the better argument", is, according to Habermas, not just an idealization or some distant utopian goal but rather a real assumption that we make a hundred times every day, as soon as we begin to speak to someone else. Even in everyday conversation we implicitly rely on the assumption that, should conflicts arise on "the level of relation", we can always voice these explicitly and "bracket" them by passing up onto the level of what Habermas calls "discourse". In the last analysis, Habermas argues, we cannot help but not just automatically assume, whenever we engage in speech with another human being, that the conversation might lead to a genuine agreement but also, indeed, that this assumption really will be borne out:

I shall develop the thesis that anyone acting communicatively must, in performing any speech-act, raise universal validity-claims and suppose that they can be vindicated.[16]

Every human being, in other words, repeatedly stubbornly assumes that his wish for mutual understanding will be fulfilled even if it remains, of course, the case that not all conversations will be such as to be carried on perfectly up to their end.

The Four Validity-Claims and The Stubborn Wish for Comprehension and Agreement

With this, we have arrived at the central idea of Habermas's philosophy. If we do indeed, both at the beginning and during the course of every conversation, assume, or implicitly raise the claim, that we should in principle be able to come to understanding and agreement with our conversation partner, then the question arises of what such an assumption or implicit claim might mean in detail. And just this is Habermas's great philosophical discovery. He applies the magnifying glass of the philosopher of language and the researcher into human communication to the beginning of "any speech-act" and investigates just what claims the participants in any conversation raise when they begin to speak or, put more precisely, what claims they must necessarily raise if what they say is to have any meaning. Anticipating a little, we may state right away that Habermas discovers precisely four universal validity-claims which every human being on earth raises, and has to raise, the moment he or she begins to speak. As Habermas puts it:

Insofar as she wants to participate in a process of reaching understanding, (a speaking individual) cannot avoid raising the following – and indeed precisely the

following – claims: she claims to be (i) uttering something *intelligibly*; (ii) giving the hearer *something* to understand; (iii) making herself thereby understandable; and (iv) coming to an understanding *with another person*.[17]

Habermas contends, then, that every one of us, as soon as we open our mouths and utter a sentence, automatically raise all four of these claims discovered by him.

The first validity-claim, we can see, is *intelligibility*. In other words, when I speak my first concern is that what I say should be understood. Consciously or unconsciously, I proceed on the assumption that I will succeed in speaking loudly and clearly enough, and in sufficiently grammatically well-formed sentences, for my conversation partners, generally speaking, to be able to understand me. Were I not to assume this, I would likely not begin to speak at all, since there would be no point in simply emitting noises that no one would understand. My first "validity-claim", then, is always: my speech-act will be a "valid" one in the basic sense of being aurally comprehensible.

The second validity-claim that, in Habermas's view, we always necessarily raise whenever we speak, concerns the content of what we say. It is always the concern of any speaker to say *something*, i.e. to pass on some informational content. I consciously or unconsciously assume, whenever I begin to speak, that I am going, through speaking, to succeed in getting across some concrete meaning-content, be it an opinion, an idea, a fact, a report on a state of affairs or whatever, which my interlocutor will recognize as such, even if he does not approve of this meaning-content or even feels strongly critical of it.

Even in such cases, he knows at least what I have said. The second validity-claim, then, runs: my speech-act will be a "valid" one in the sense of having conveyed *something*, of having "gotten *something* across".

The third validity-claim relates to my sincerity or, as Habermas puts it, to the subjective "truthfulness" (something, as we shall see, distinct from the objective "truth") of my act of speech. In other words: one of my essential (conscious or unconscious) concerns in every conversation is whether or not what I say corresponds to what I really think, i.e. whether I am really bound by it, as opposed to its merely being something I am saying without really inwardly believing. The third validity-claim, then, runs: I always consciously or unconsciously assume that, whenever I begin to speak, others will on their side assume that whatever I say is my actual, frank and honest view and is not a lie or something I have randomly invented. In other words, I implicitly assume that I will be taken to be a truthful person who, in expressing himself, really does express *himself*, his own opinion, and not some opinion he merely pretends to hold.

The fourth and final validity-claim, however, relates indeed to the *truth* (in distinction from the mere "truthfulness") of what I say. It relates, in other words, to the general validity in the sense of the *correctness* of my statement. A speaker always wishes, consciously or unconsciously, that whatever he says should be, generally speaking, *true and cor-*

rect. This fourth and last validity-claim is thus perhaps the highest and most demanding. I wish, in the last analysis, not only that the things I say should be expressed comprehensibly (1st validity-claim), should have some graspable content (2nd validity-claim), and should correspond to what I actually inwardly believe (3rd validity-claim). No, above and beyond all this I wish also that the things I say in the course of a conversation should be such as to count as "true and correct". Which is to say that, ideally, all the people I converse with should be able either to confirm, along with me, what I am saying as "correct", agree with me about it, and share a commonly acknowledged "truth" with me, or, in the case where their perspective is such that they find themselves unable to agree with me, should be able to engage in discourse and discussion with me about the truth-content of what I am saying for as long as it takes to arrive at some shared idea of "truth". In any case, however, the fourth validity-claim runs: I wish to count as someone who makes a proposal regarding what is "true and correct" and who engages thereby with other people's proposals regarding what is "true and correct" in such a way as to aim at arriving at a shared idea of truth.

In sum, then, and in their mutual effect on one another, these four validity-claims which we automatically raise in every conversation aim at the "bringing about of an agreement". Habermas explicitly states that

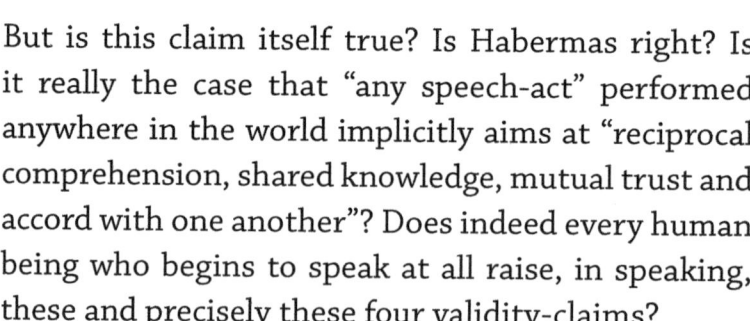

The aim of reaching understanding is to bring about an agreement that terminates in the intersubjective mutuality of reciprocal comprehension, shared knowledge, mutual trust and accord with one

another. Agreement is based on recognition of the four corresponding validity claims: comprehensibility, truth, truthfulness and rightness.[18]

But is this claim itself true? Is Habermas right? Is it really the case that "any speech-act" performed anywhere in the world implicitly aims at "reciprocal comprehension, shared knowledge, mutual trust and accord with one another"? Does indeed every human being who begins to speak at all raise, in speaking, these and precisely these four validity-claims?

"Am I Driving Here or You?" – The Four Validity-Claims in Everyday Speech

This discovery of Habermas's certainly is a challenging and exciting one. In order to test its validity I asked the participants in a philosophy seminar to come up with some phrase that they had used in some real conversation or everyday interaction so that we could analyze together whether it really did implicitly contain the four validity-claims evoked by Habermas.

Many different suggestions were forthcoming. Then a female participant mentioned, with a smile, that she had had occasion a few days previously, when she had been out for a drive with her boyfriend, to utter the phrase "am I driving here or you?" This example produced a ripple of laughter in the seminar room because, particularly in the German-speaking world in which this story I'm telling takes place, this phrase is associated rather with sarcasm and even with good-natured conflict, so that it seems, at first sight, to do the very opposite to confirming a theory like Habermas's, whereby speech is always oriented to mutual understanding and agreement. The whole class, however, was immediately in agreement that we should try to analyze above all a phrase like this in terms of Habermas's implicit validity-claims, since Habermas had, indeed, explicitly contended that these latter, being universal, could be detected to be present in absolutely every speech-act.

We began by writing the four Habermasian validity-claims once again up on the blackboard:

- uttering something *intelligible*
- giving the hearer *something* to understand
- making *oneself* understood thereby
- coming to an understanding with *another person*.[19]

The first of these claims – uttering something intelligible – posed, in this case, no problem. We had to concede to Habermas that the speech-act "am I driving here or you?" which we had undertaken to examine was one in which this claim was certainly fulfilled. The young woman, indeed, emphasized that she had made her meaning quite especially clear and intelligible to her boyfriend, enunciating her question loudly and clearly so that there was hardly any possibility of him mishearing or miscomprehending it. Habermas's first criterion for a valid speech-act was, then, in this case definitely met.

Then we moved on to discuss the second validity-claim: that of "giving the hearer something to understand". Had the young woman, with this utterance, "given her boyfriend to understand *something*" in the sense in which Habermas argues a speech-act must "give something to understand"? And if so, what exactly had this "something" been? This, we soon realized, was not so simple a question as the first. On a first, very literal and superficial examination what the young woman was doing was just asking her boyfriend about the simple matter of physical fact: which of us is sitting in the driver's seat right now, you or me? And since the physical fact was indeed that she was physically located in the driver's seat and her boyfriend next to her in the passenger seat, her boyfriend could surely only reply: "you".

But the participants in the seminar were soon able to establish, by discussion, that the "something" that the young woman had given her boyfriend to understand with this utterance went, in fact, far beyond this simple piece of information about the physical world. What she "gave him to understand" by saying what she did was really that he should stop nagging at her while she was driving and should keep his "mansplaining" comments and instructions to himself. What really mattered to the young woman in this moment and this situation was that her boyfriend should become aware that he was behaving, in her view, quite wrongly. Since the boyfriend really had no option but to answer, inwardly, the clearly rhetorical question "am I driving or are you?" with a "you", he must surely himself have grasped what he was "being given to understand". What he was being made mindful of was that he did not have the right, as a "backseat driver", to "mansplain" to the young woman actually driving the vehicle how she ought to go about her task, as this was serving no purpose other than to make her nervous. This speech-act, then, did indubitably also raise the second of Habermas's validity-claims since, as the young woman herself pointed out in concluding her remarks on this point: "you can be damn sure he understood the point I was trying to get across."

The same goes for Habermas's third validity-claim. As everyone in the seminar had to agree, the young woman had not only made *herself* understood with this utterance but had done so in especially clear and emphatic form. She had, in other words, expressed her own individual person in the most authentic way through this speech-act and had left her boyfriend in no doubt that the wish to be left in peace to do her driving was a real and sincerely held desire on her part. In other words, the speech-act definitely did meet the criterion of "truthfulness". The young woman herself stated that the cowed silence that was her boyfriend's only reply to this rhetorical question: "am I driving here or are you?" was indication enough that he had become wary of saying the wrong thing and of thereby "pouring oil on the fire". In other words, her boyfriend had been left in no doubt that she "meant it", i.e. that what she was expressing was quite sincere.

There remained, then, only the fourth validity-claim: the claim that a speech-act implies a coming to an understanding *with another person*. The seminar's discussion of this part of the question went on, of course, the longest. One participant, for example, was very strongly of the opinion that the speech-act in question neither raised nor fulfilled this fourth of the supposedly "universal" validity-claims ascribed by Habermas to every speech-act, so that Habermas's philosophy would be shown, by this concrete example, to be a fundamentally misguided one. Because, so this participant argued, it had certainly been no part of the young woman's intention, in uttering this rhetorical question: "am I driving here or are you?" to come to an understanding *with* someone by mutual *exchange* of views. Rather her speech-act had been of a unilateral, even of a dictatorial nature: an abrupt instruction that he should hold his tongue. In other words, it had been a command which neither invited nor allowed any "intersubjectivity". She had, so ran this participant's interpretation of the incident, simply ordered her boyfriend to shut up, in a one-sided, egocentric exercise of power, as indeed often occurs in love relationships when things are going some way that doesn't suit the female partner and when a woman, for once in her life, finds herself having to deal with criticism of her behaviour.

This decidedly male perspective on the episode of language-mediated interaction produced the same sort of laughter in the seminar room as had the initial proposal that this particular speech-act be the one to be analyzed. But the contention was not uninteresting. Because it is indeed Habermas's argument that the implicit validity-claim of a "coming to an understanding *with another person*" necessarily aims at "an agreement *jointly or commonly* arrived at" and never just at one person's dictatorially forcing the compliance of another.

But then the discussion took a new turn. One especially enthusiastic female participant chimed in and argued that "what this man just said is complete nonsense and could only come from a distorted male perspective on the incident". The question "am I driving here or are you?" had, so argued the new contributor to the discussion, nothing at all about it of an "egocentric, dictatorial command". On the contrary, even if it had been posed in a challenging tone and manner it remained, in the end, just a question. The boyfriend, so this new participant in the discussion went on, could easily have given either an affirmative or a negative response to this question. If, for example, he had replied that, while not wishing to overstep any boundaries and fully appreciating his girlfriend's driving, he had thought that, since he was perhaps the more experienced motorist and also perhaps knew the area better than her, she might on her side appreciate a few tips and pieces of advice, this response might easily have led to a constructive discussion and exchange of views. And even if there had been no more discussion and her boyfriend had simply said that he was sorry and that he would be more considerate in future, this would also surely have counted as an agreement arrived at through communication in the sense intended by Habermas.

Thus, there certainly had been made here, this new participant in the seminar went on, a genuine offer of conversational interaction even if the question had sounded merely rhetorical. This offer concerned the question of whether or not the young man was going to accord to his girlfriend a proper recognition of her role as driver instead of just passing the matter off with a placatory "OK, dear". Even if the young man in the passenger seat had just fallen silent or had, as men tend often to do on such occasions, tried to joke his way out of the situation, it would still remain the case that the young woman had been aiming, with her question, at coming to some agreement with him regarding the recognition due to her role as driver of the car, given that she would certainly accord him this same recognition were he sitting in her place. In the view of this second female participant in the seminar, then, the speech-act in question had certainly involved also Habermas's fourth type of validity-claim. The young woman had very definitely assumed, with her utterance, that the question needed to be, and would be, resolved between her and her boyfriend of whether whoever was driving the car at any time had a right, that needed to be respected, to decide for themselves all arising questions of driving technique and handling of the traffic.

The participants in the seminar then enquired of the initial speaker how things had in fact developed in the course of her drive with her boyfriend. She replied as follows: "He did, in fact, after thinking about it for a little while, try to pass things off with a joke and said that it was really only very rarely that he said anything, namely when he became anxious about our safety. Of course, I immediately asked him if he didn't feel safe with me driving and whether he was aware of how insulting such an idea was for me. He then assured me that it really wasn't his own safety that he was worried about, only mine, because he loved me so much, but just because this was so he would do his best not to make such comments in future, except when it really looked like I was about to run a red light or something." "And did he keep to this commitment?" asked another female participant in the seminar. "Yes, during that particular drive he did," replied the young woman, "and I think he will continue to do better in future – although he is an awful Neanderthal." Once again, there was much laughter in the seminar.

The result of our analysis, however, was clear to everyone. This question "am I driving here or are you?" does indeed implicitly raise also the fourth of the validity-claims discovered by Habermas: namely, the claim, or aspiration, to come to an understanding *with another person*. To sum up, then: Habermas is not wrong in holding that, even in such a trivial speech-act performed in an everyday situation as asking "am I driving here or are you?", there are present all four of those "universal validity-claims" which tend, together, to bring about a situation of mutual agreement. Let us recall:

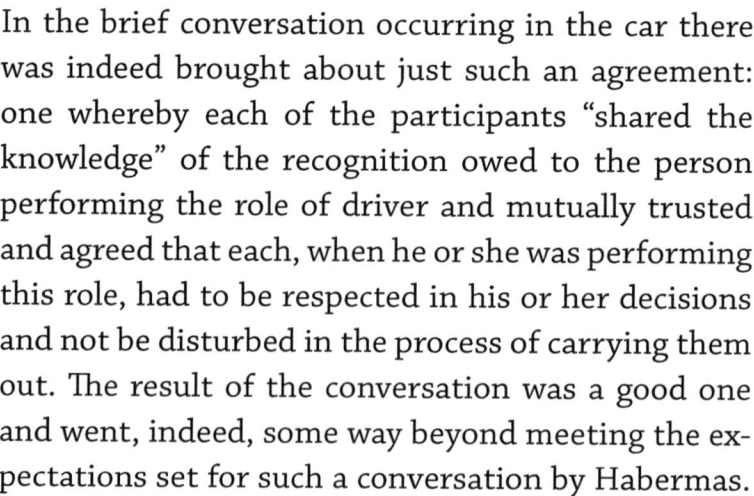

The aim of reaching understanding is to bring about an agreement which terminates in the intersubjective mutuality of
- reciprocal comprehension
- shared knowledge
- mutual trust
- and accord with one another.[20]

In the brief conversation occurring in the car there was indeed brought about just such an agreement: one whereby each of the participants "shared the knowledge" of the recognition owed to the person performing the role of driver and mutually trusted and agreed that each, when he or she was performing this role, had to be respected in his or her decisions and not be disturbed in the process of carrying them out. The result of the conversation was a good one and went, indeed, some way beyond meeting the expectations set for such a conversation by Habermas.

Because Habermas, of course, does not go so far as to claim that absolutely "any speech-act" will lead, or must lead, to mutual agreement. He claims only that human beings, as soon as they begin to speak, implicitly presuppose, through the four validity-claims necessarily raised by their speech, the possibility of such an agreement. Whether such an agreement is, in each case, actually reached is a question that Habermas leaves open.

It appears, then, that Habermas's discovery that human beings generally raise, when speaking with one another, these four validity-claims is a sound one. But what about the particular case of the liar? The liar, indeed, wishes to utter something intelligible (1st validity-claim), and to give his hearer "something to understand" (2nd validity-claim). He fulfils, however, at best only in very distorted form the third and fourth of Habermas's validity-claims, which stipulate a making oneself understood and a coming to an understanding with another person, because, with his lie, he in fact conceals himself and his true opinion and, rather than attempting to come to any real agreement about the truth with other people, his aim is to deceive them as to the truth. Habermas concedes that this is the case but argues, rightly, that a conscious lie is an exception that proves the rule.

But what is it that Habermas is really trying to convey to us with this notion of four universal validity-claims? The vision he evokes is certainly an interesting one but appears, in the last analysis, not really to amount to any great philosophical discovery. But appearances here are deceptive. That every speaking person all over the world raises, with every speech-act, these four and precisely these four validity-claims is in fact something that has enormous consequences and ramifications.

Because, so Habermas concludes, if, firstly, all human beings everywhere raise, each time they speak, claims to "intelligibility, truth, truthfulness and correctness" and if, secondly, these four claims together aim at agreement consisting in "reciprocal comprehension, shared knowledge, mutual trust and accord with one another", then we must say that there inheres in language a profound tendency to "understanding based on good reasons". But "understanding based on good reasons" is nothing other or less than the ancient ideal of "reason" or "rationality" itself. Habermas, therefore, speaks of a "communicative rationality" and a "communicative action" that follows directly from that faculty of language that defines the human species itself.

Rationality as the Goal of Every Act of Linguistic Understanding

We thus find ourselves at the very core and epicentre of Habermas's philosophical discovery. Habermas shows us that human history is pervaded, from the very beginning, by this "communicative reason" or "communicative rationality". From his earliest origins on, Habermas argues, Man has had an "interest in autonomy and responsibility" inseparable from an interest in coming to an agreement. Moreover, this interest in forming the world to fit the demands of reason is not just a pipe-dream or "mere idea":

> The human interest in autonomy and responsibility is not mere fancy for it can be apprehended a priori. What raises us out of Nature is […] language.

> Through its structure autonomy and responsibility are posited for us. Our first sentence expresses unequivocally the intention of universal and unconstrained consensus.[21]

Our making ourselves understood to one another through language, then, implicitly aims, considered across the whole course of human history, at a "universal and unconstrained consensus", a universal agreement among all human beings. But how, concretely, is this to be envisaged? Does it mean that there will exist, one day, on our planet a true "world society" in which all human beings, regardless of nationality, culture, poverty or wealth, will all be agreed upon certain rules for living together as one? Will our "communicative rationality" develop ever farther in this direction over time? Habermas's vision is, in fact, a vision somewhat along these lines:

> There is, inarguably, a certain intellectual motif and basic intuition that has always guided my work: namely, the idea that forms and ways of living together might be found through which individual autonomy and

> the dependence of individuals on one another could be peacefully reconciled [...] This intuition [...] aims at the experience of an

undamaged intersubjectivity [...] It is a question of an amity that does not, indeed, exclude all conflict. What is at issue is rather developing human structures and practices through which conflict can be survived.[22]

These four sentences reflect the core idea of Habermas's philosophy and at the same time its emancipatory message. His most basic concern is an "undamaged intersubjectivity". This "undamaged intersubjectivity" is still very far, indeed, from being brought to realization. But it exists, Habermas believes, as an inherent goal in all human language and inter-human communication. And this means that, as human language develops, human history too, despite all its setbacks and disasters, tends to follow a slow but steady upward path.

We have the capacity, Habermas argues, to free ourselves, to an extent at least, from our animal origins, our brute aggressions, and even from the mutual exploitation that characterizes capitalism and to settle our conflicts, henceforth, in a genuinely humane form. Because history is not, as Nietzsche had contended, merely an "eternal return of the same".

Nor does it consist in an inevitably graver and graver alienation of Man both from outer and from his own inner Nature, as was feared by Habermas's own teachers Adorno and Horkheimer. Contrarily to both these views, Habermas is convinced that the course of human history provides a real chance for humanity's development toward Reason:

I believe that I am able to show that a species the preservation of whose material existence must inevitably pass through structures of mutual linguistic understanding is placed thereby in a

necessary relation to the ideal of reason. In the validity-claims by which we are obliged, however implicitly, to orient ourselves when we act communicatively there inheres a stubborn, even if constantly suppressed, claim to rationality.[23]

This "stubborn claim to rationality" can lead to the development of rational ways of resolving conflict all over the world. This development of communicative reason, however, should not be taken to be something that can be left to happen by itself. At least implicitly, Habermas urges us to contribute, wherever possible, to the rational solution of problems by attempting to come, through discourse, to an understanding with others. Such an understanding, as we have seen, is already hypothetically inherent in the four validity-claims; we can ourselves, however, always make a contribution to its actual realization. We can do this by adopting the general practice of communicating in an open, trusting and above all uncoercive manner with other human beings. A model or ideal for such a practice is what Habermas calls "domination-free discourse".

Domination-Free Discourse and Discourse Ethics

This postulate of a "domination-free discourse" is one which has become known worldwide through Habermas's work and it will most likely always be associated with his name. It surely forms the heart of his whole philosophy. Because these two words sum up, on the one hand, the critically emancipatory impulse of his thought and, on the other, its speech-pragmatic aspect related to the history of the species. They are a thorn in the side of every dictatorial, undemocratic or authoritarian form of organization, be the organization in question a society, a political party or a family.

For example, if a father responds negatively to some wish expressed by his growing son by saying: "So long as you're living under my roof, you're to do as I say, is that clear?", this sort of "coming to an understanding" is certainly not to be described as "domination-free discourse" but is rather a clear case of authoritarian exercise of power. It can lead, therefore, to no genuine or, as Habermas would put it, "unconstrained" consensus. But that the consensus should be unconstrained is precisely the issue. We should, argues Habermas, ideally and whenever this is possible "with a perception that is independent of every field trust to the non-constraining constraint of the better argument" and never simply to the exercise of power.

With perfect logical consistency Habermas connects this, his ethical demand for a "domination-free discourse", to the four validity-claims that he had discovered to be implicit in all speech. In order to really vitally fulfil the four claims to "intelligibility, truth, truthfulness and correctness" which we implicitly raise in every conversation the particular conversation in question needs to be one which we conduct free of fear or of intimidation by the power, rank or reputation of our interlocutor. For this to be the case certain prior conditions must be met. As Habermas himself states:

Ideal speech situations must fulfil certain conditions.[24]

He defines four hypothetical conditions apt to guarantee a coming to an understanding specifically in the mode of domination-free discourse, thus ensuring that all participants in a conversation can actually bring to realization the four implicit validity-claims. The first condition consists in the following: that the participants in the conversation put aside all their thinking in terms of power and status; or alternatively, and preferably of course, that these participants should all find themselves from the very start on an equal level with one another so that all can discourse with one another from like to like:

Admitted to participation in such a discourse will be those speakers alone who have, as agents, equal chances to engage in regulative speech-acts: i.e. to give orders or to refuse them, to permit or

to forbid, to make or to accept promises, to give or to receive guarantees etc.[25]

Participants, in other words, must ideally be people enjoying absolutely equal rights. This should be the case not only as regards their positions of power but also as regards their abilities to express themselves and make themselves understood. If this latter condition were not fulfilled, then it could be that a skilled speaker would acquire a significant advantage in communicating and achieving his needs:

All potential participants in a discourse must have equal opportunity to perform communicative speech-acts so that they are, at any time, able either to initiate such a discourse or carry it on by means of question and answer, speech and counter-speech.[26]

A second necessary precondition for the existence of an ideal, domination-free discourse in which "the better argument" alone counts is that all participants should have an equal ability to justify and support with reasons the arguments that they bring into the conversation and that they should likewise have an equal ability to judge, and even to refute, the validity of the arguments brought by others as well as the reasons offered in support of these:

All participants in discourse must have an equal opportunity and ability to propose interpretations, assertions, recommendations, explanations and justifications, as well as to call into question, legitimate or refute the claims to validity represented by these latter, so that no pre-conceived opinion is spared, for very long, exposure to critique.[27]

The fourth and last precondition for the coming into being of a domination-free discourse or "ideal speech situation" is the following: all participants must have an equal capacity to introduce into the conversation in an equally clear and comprehensible manner their emotional states and the urgency of their wishes, or in other words of their feelings, fears and dreams:

Admitted to participation in such a discourse will be those speakers alone who have, as agents, equal chances to engage also in

representative speech-acts: i.e. to give expression to their attitudes, feelings and intentions.[28]

In summary, then, one can say that domination-free discourse represents an ideal speech situation which one will seldom, indeed, encounter in real life in so pure a form as this but which can be taken as a sort of standard or criterion by which to establish and assess the degree of emancipation existing within a family, a social group, or an entire society. To do this, one needs only to compare any real conversation, or any real process of decision within society, with the ideal speech situation, asking: "do the partners in the communication going on within a family, a group, an organization or a whole society enjoy equal rights with one another or do they not? Do all have the same possibilities of self-expression? Is the communication a symmetrical one? Are decisions arrived at through "the non-constraining constraint of the better argument" or rather through power and violence? How closely does the situation of the speakers approximate to the ideal speech situation and in what respects does it fall far short?"

Habermas himself emphasizes this point that the ideal speech situation is a notion of great importance even if one would seek in vain for any perfect instantiation of it in the real world:

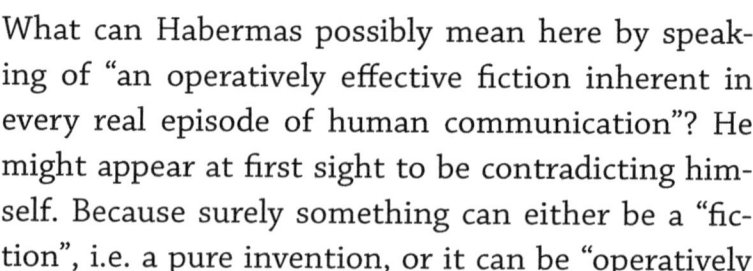

The ideal speech situation is neither an empirical phenomenon nor a mere ideal construct. Rather, it is an assumption which we unavoidably reciprocally make whenever we enter into any form of discourse with another person. It is, in other words, an operatively effective fiction inherent in every real episode of human communication.[29]

What can Habermas possibly mean here by speaking of "an operatively effective fiction inherent in every real episode of human communication"? He might appear at first sight to be contradicting himself. Because surely something can either be a "fiction", i.e. a pure invention, or it can be "operatively effective in real communication". How, though, can it be both at once? In other words, how can something that is admitted not to exist be "operatively effective"? But Habermas's meaning is in fact quite coherent and consistent. His point is that, although the ideal speech situation with its four conditions for domination-free discourse may be in our everyday conversations a mere fiction to which nothing real corresponds, we are nonetheless obliged, as soon as we begin to engage in human communication, to assume that this ideal speech situation could, in principle, be achieved. It is something present to our minds whenever we speak, whether we will it to be or not. For this reason, this conscious or unconscious human attitude of expectation, which is indeed to be encountered in every conversation conducted anywhere in the world, proves, though "fictional", to be effective after all and tends to influence these conversations positively in the sense of nudging them toward their inherent aim of mutual understanding and agreement.

By pointing this out, however, Habermas also raises the more strictly philosophically methodological claim that his "discourse ethics" represent more than just a proposal posited as a desirable ideal, i.e. more than just an arbitrary construction that he, as an individual thinker, has plucked, with his imagination, out of the air. Rather, suggests Habermas, the ideal speech situation is something structurally built into all language; something the real effectiveness of which can be proven by looking at things from the point of view of what Habermas calls "universal pragmatics":

> It belongs to the very structure of any possible act of speech that, in performing it, we behave, counter-factually, as if the ideal speech situation were not just a fiction but already a reality.[30]

The word "ethics" comes from Ancient Greek and means "moral action" or "an orientation of one's action by reference to the morally good". As a result of our discussion we can recognize that Habermas, with his "discourse ethics" and "ideal speech situation", is not laying down any concrete and substantial moral stipulations for his readers. We do not, for example, find in Habermas anything so concrete as the famous Biblical moral stipulations: "thou shalt not steal" or "thou shalt honour thy father and thy mother". Instead of this, what Habermas has developed is a "formal" or "procedural" principle that helps us to make good moral decisions. In other words, he has done something similar to what Kant did two hundred years before him. In Kant's case ethical action was defined by the famous "categorical imperative" which ran: "you should act in such a way that you can wish that the maxim of your action, i.e. the principle on which it is based, can count as the principle of the action of all human beings and can be applied as such". In other words, Kant argued that the principle guiding one's own actions should, ideally, be such a perfect one that it could be elevated to the status of a universal law. The Kantian text here actually runs: "So act that the maxim of your will could always hold at the same time as a principle in the giving of a universal law."[31]

Habermas has now added to this "categorical imperative" something which is, in his own view at least, quite decisive: namely, this consideration of "domination-free discourse". Where the linguistic paradigm and the particular specifications of his "discourse ethics" are added into the equation Kant's "categorical imperative" would need to be revised and expanded so as to run: "If there is a maxim that

you consider to be a good one and a good orientation for action and that you would like to see become
a maxim also for the actions of others, you should,
before attempting to realize this, discuss the matter
with these others and thereby come to agreement
about a shared maxim common to all." Habermas,
indeed, proposes just this, writing that:

> Rather than ascribing as valid to all
> others any maxim that I can will to
> be a universal law, I must submit
> my maxim to all others for purposes
> of discursively testing its claim to
> universality.[32]

Were society really organized in the spirit of discourse ethics, every law that was passed would, ideally, first be discussed, and its letter and substance
carefully discursively agreed on, by all those citizens
who might potentially be affected by it. Habermas's
discourse ethics, then, attempts to expand Kant's
idea of a "categorical imperative" as the highest moral
law by adding to it the dimension of intersubjectivity:

The emphasis shifts from what each can will without contradiction to be a general law to what all can will in agreement to be a universal norm.[33]

The core of Habermas's ethics, then, is the bringing into being of a "domination-free discourse" and of intersubjectivity as a warranty for moral decisions.

The Development of Humanity Within the Linguistic Paradigm

At the beginning of his principal philosophical work, *The Theory of Communicative Action*, Habermas issues an appeal for a radical change in our ways of thinking. He even speaks of a "paradigm shift" in our way of looking at world history and the development of reason.

"Paradigm" is a word derived from classical Greek and means "model". Habermas argues, then, that

65

when one proceeds on the basis of the "model of language" and focuses on that communicative rationality which develops out of language one has no choice but to look at world history in a completely new way.

The "paradigm", or model, on the basis of which Habermas's own teachers, Adorno and Horkheimer, had proceeded had been the analysis of instrumental reason alone and of the role of instrumental action in human history. Marx, from whom they took their inspiration, had done much the same. Marx, Adorno and Horkheimer, in other words, had all focused on analyzing the ways in which, since time immemorial, human beings had tried to survive and how, specifically, they had done this by bringing Nature more and more under human control by means of improved technology and new production methods, thus achieving more and more of their purely instrumental goals. Habermas, however, sees this as a hopelessly one-sided approach. He recommends an entirely new perspective:

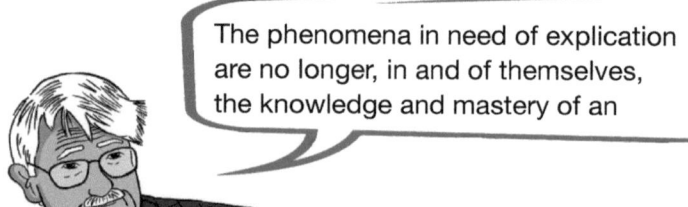

The phenomena in need of explication are no longer, in and of themselves, the knowledge and mastery of an

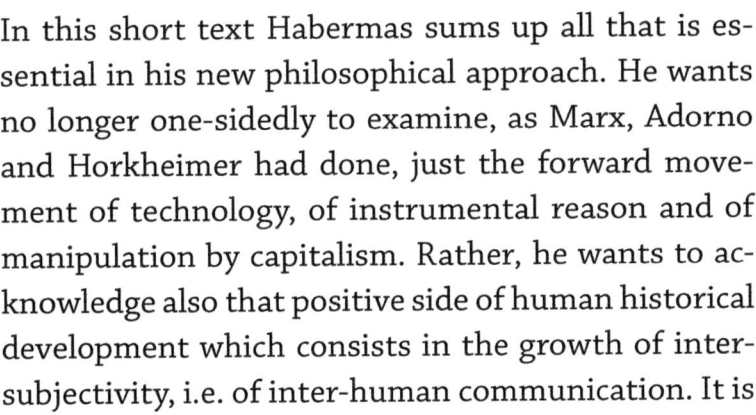

objective Nature but the intersubjectivity of possible understanding and agreement [...] The focus of investigation therefore shifts from cognitive-instrumental rationality to communicative rationality. And what is

paradigmatic for the latter is not the relation of a solitary subject to something in the objective world that can be represented and manipulated but the intersubjective relation that speaking and acting subjects take up when they come to an understanding with one another about something.[34]

In this short text Habermas sums up all that is essential in his new philosophical approach. He wants no longer one-sidedly to examine, as Marx, Adorno and Horkheimer had done, just the forward movement of technology, of instrumental reason and of manipulation by capitalism. Rather, he wants to acknowledge also that positive side of human historical development which consists in the growth of intersubjectivity, i.e. of inter-human communication. It is now of primary importance, Habermas contends, to finally philosophically investigate this second important possibility which exists in the sphere of human action – a possibility which has hitherto been left largely in darkness:

This means [...] a change of paradigm within action theory from goal-directed to communicative action [...].[35]

Our task today, argues Habermas, is to try to understand communicative action and communicative reason and to take advantage of the possibilities these offer. These possibilities, he insists, are far from insignificant. Because those "validity claims" inherent in language which we have examined above, and the claim to the fulfilment of the promise of Reason which shines forth in them, have the potential to bring about nothing less than a sort of utopia: namely, the utopia of an unforced intersubjectivity which will, perhaps, in the end, make possible an uncoerced understanding and agreement between all human beings all over the world:

The structures of reason [...] become accessible to analysis when the ideas of reconciliation and freedom are deciphered as codes for a form of intersubjectivity, however utopian it may be, that makes possible a mutual and constraint-free understanding among individuals in their dealings with one another as well as the identity of individuals who come to a compulsion-free understanding with themselves: sociation without repression.[36]

But the unfolding of communicative reason or, as Habermas puts it, communicative rationality is not, in fact, a utopia. Rather, it is recognizable as really present in history and can potentially really lead to a world permanently at peace. We would, indeed, in such a world still be bound and obliged to one another by discursively-agreed laws and rules. We would, however, no longer experience this as any sort of compulsion but rather as, in Habermas's phrase:

[…] Sociation without repression.[37]

This development toward a happier form of human socialization than our history has hitherto known is, as we have said, something inherent in the language we use to live our lives:

Through (language's) structure autonomy and responsibility are posited for us. Our first sentence expresses unequivocally the intention of universal and unconstrained consensus.[38]

But if autonomy and responsibility, and communicative rationality, "are posited for us" and if, secondly, the intention of an unconstrained consensus is inherent in language itself, then the question necessarily arises: why has communicative rationality not already flourished more fully in the course of human history up until now? Why are there still wars? Why do individuals and nations appear to practice so rarely in their dealings with one another a "domination-free discourse" and why do we still find, in so many areas, instead of an "unconstrained consensus", repression and exploitation? Habermas himself, however, has asked himself these very questions.

Communicative vs. Instrumental Reason

There exists unfortunately in history, Habermas recognizes, a certain persistent countervailing force to that force of communicative reason which is the focus of his own thought. This countervailing force is not, indeed, anything so grand or metaphysical as "the devil" or some other "spirit of Evil". It is simply that "instrumental reason" on which we have already touched and which is ineradicably part of human nature. This means, put very simply, that what we do is often not at all that which we have recognized, through conversation with others, to be the right thing but rather that which seems to us to be easiest and most advantageous for our own selves.

Another term that Habermas uses for this latter, self-serving behaviour is "strategic reason". Already in his early essays from the 1960s and early 70s, such as *Theory and Practice*, he points out how this sort of action plays a significant role in our lives:

> To the extent that our actions are governed by those systems geared essentially to technical progress, we may say that they follow a model of strategic, or instrumental, action.[39]

In what does the great distinction between instrumental and communicative action actually consist? Certainly, in our everyday contacts with friends and family it is "communicative action" that predominates. Here, there is constantly a lively exchange of views, occurring via language. People discuss with one another, coming to agreements about what we plan to do together or about what sorts of rules are to govern our time spent together. It is decided, for example, by discussion who is to do the dishes or the laundry, who is to clean the house or take out the garbage, where and when one wants to go on holiday and such matters. Habermas calls this sphere of our lives "the lifeworld" and recognizes that this "lifeworld" tends to be characterized predominantly and from the very start by communicative action:

> The lifeworld is, so to speak, the transcendental site where speaker and hearer meet, where they can reciprocally raise claims that their utterances fit the world (objective, social or subjective) and where they can criticize or confirm those validity claims, settle their disagreements, and arrive at agreements.[40]

Habermas's description of the lifeworld here sounds rather abstract. He speaks of it as a "transcendental site" where "speakers and hearers" meet and "raise claims that their utterances fit the world". But underneath the abstract philosophical terminology all he is saying is that when we meet and talk together with, for example, family or friends this is an occasion for us to test and assure ourselves, each with the help of the others, whether our wishes, cares and fears about ourselves and the world around us are in fact wishes, cares and fears that others can understand and relate to or whether in thinking, wishing or fearing as we do we are in fact "barking up the wrong tree" or living in some fantasy world of our own.

Only through contact and conversation with others, says Habermas, can we discover whether the picture we have formed of ourselves and of the world is a correct or rather a false and distorted one. There may well, indeed, arise a "dissensus" in the course of such conversations, with opinions on these questions proving to be different or entirely contrary. They may confirm one in one's own view of oneself and the world; alternatively, this view may have to be revised so radically that there is a risk of one's feeling offended; and a third possibility is that one may arrive, through exchange of viewpoints, at a new, shared consensus. All these results are possible. But one thing is unshakeably the case: it is only through a living encounter with others in the lifeworld that we can possibly acquire any reliable sense of what is real and what is not.

Habermas's talk of the lifeworld as the site of "the raising of validity-claims", of "the settling of disagreements" and of "the arriving at agreements" can also be expressed in less solemn and formal terms. He means to say simply that in the lifeworld of friendly and family relations we can be ourselves and say whatever is on our mind. We can, indeed, disagree with others but on a basis of mutual trust. We can dispute, be reconciled and perhaps in the end come to a common understanding.

I still remember very well the attempts of my partner and I, both of whom were working full-time, to bring our three boys, all of school age, to take a more active part in maintaining the household. We sat around a table and spoke with them about how we might organize, in future, a fair division of household tasks within the family. It was a matter simply of such trivial things as doing the dishes, vacuuming, taking out the garbage etc. The discussion was a passionate one, with the boys presenting, with the tendency to exaggeration typical for their age, arguments to the effect that their other "commitments" allowed them only limited leeway for participation in such activities or were even so demanding on their time and energy that they ruled out such cooperation altogether. Their schoolwork would suffer, they argued, and reinforced this with the further point that their social lives would suffer even more. In other households, they contended, no such demands were made on the children – a fact, they suggested, which might be taken to put our demand that they do the dishes occasionally in the category of infringement of their basic human right to equal treatment. On the other hand, however, the boys did show, right from the start, some degree of understanding for, and even agreement with, the idea that my partner and I's "validity-claims" were justified when we pointed out that we should not, after our hard working days, have to take on the tasks of washing, cleaning and shopping not just for us two but for all five members of the household.

In the end we arrived at an agreement which all five of us found acceptable. Each of the three boys took on the task of loading, on a specific weekday, the dirty dishes into the dishwasher and also scrubbed the larger pots and pans – an amount of work equivalent to a contribution to the collective family welfare of one hour a week. My partner and I took on the same duties for one weekday each and also at the weekend. Each person vacuumed in their own private room and took out that room's garbage. But the vacuuming and taking out of the rubbish from the rooms used by us all was, once again, a task taken on by my partner and I. As you can see, the agreement on division of labour that we arrived at was not exactly a model of equality and fairness. Nonetheless, we had succeeded in arriving at some sort of real consensus.

In the professional and economic spheres, however, such solutions arrived at purely by discussion are relatively rarely met with. In these spheres, points out Habermas, it is instrumental, or "strategic", reason and action that predominate: i.e. an action oriented to the achievement of fixed ends that, as a rule, leaves no place for discussion. What matters in these spheres is to "produce", swiftly and efficiently, to outdo the competition, and to achieve the once-set goals in the way that involves the minimum expenditure. A strategic action counts as a "good action" wherever it proves itself to be effective in actual empirical practice. Although industry and commerce sometimes like to portray themselves as functioning only through "teamwork" the fact is that in these spheres there are and have always been strict hierarchical structures governing every decision and appointed "deciders" who cannot afford to be open to debate. Indeed, even these "deciders" enjoy very little leeway for their decisions, since they are obliged constantly to obey imperatives arising from the realities of production, marketing and sales. These technically-guided strategic decisions made in commerce and industry are different in their fundamental nature from those agreements come to, in the lifeworld, via intersubjective dialogue:

> Whereas the acceptance of technical rules and strategies is dependent upon the validity of empirically true or analytically correct propositions, the acceptability of social norms is grounded solely in the intersubjectivity of agreement about intentions and secured only by general recognition.[41]

This distinction between a technical-instrumental thinking within the world of the "system" and a communicative thinking and acting, based on general agreement and recognition of norms, within the "lifeworld" is a distinction that has a historical dimension. This dichotomy, argues Habermas, has existed since the beginning of human history. These two ways of thinking and acting characterize humanity since time immemorial and continue to characterize our species today.

In the speech, entitled *Knowledge and Human Interests*, with which he accepted his appointment to a professorship at Frankfurt University, the birthplace of Critical Theory, Habermas explained to his listeners that human history rests upon a simultaneous development both of communicative and of instrumental reason. Not only have human beings since earliest prehistory agreed rules of behaviour, customs and taboos with one another; they have also, this whole time, been equally urgently interested in appropriating Nature and gaining power over it through knowledge and control.

But what does it mean to "appropriate and control Nature"? By this Habermas simply means that, in order to survive, human beings must eat and drink and that they have an interest in seeing to it that these needs are met as efficiently as possible. We human beings, then, have from the beginning always asked ourselves such instrumentally rational questions as what strategies and methods should be used in order to hunt best, raise the best crops, breed the best animals and generally to survive and dwell most comfortably in the world. Since, however, such activities as speaking with one another and exchanging views and opinions have also been features of our human life right from that point on when we can first genuinely be described as "humans", we have also, from the very beginning, had an interest in maintaining and developing structures of communication and communicative action. These two "knowledge-interests", i.e. the technical-strategic and the linguistic-communicative, were, Habermas argues, not biologically inborn in human beings. They emerge, however, directly out of the life-conditions which already the earliest human beings must have found themselves faced with and under which they had to survive:

Knowledge-interests [...] arise out of imperatives of that socio-cultural life-form which is bound at once to work and to language.[42]

One might initially be tempted to conclude that this dichotomy or duality which, as Habermas claims, has characterized human life for as long as we have been truly human is a very good and sensible thing. Depending what needs to be done at any particular moment, we act either in technical-instrumental or, alternatively, in communicative-interactive fashion. There have been throughout history, we might say, two different "building sites" on which we human beings have been working, using on each a different "set of tools". Whereas on the "building site" of our private and social lives we collectively produce, using the tools of communicative action, the norms and rules of behaviour for our co-existence with one another, on our lives' other "building site", namely economic and commercial existence, we employ rather the "toolbox" of instrumental, goal-oriented rationality and are constantly concerned to optimize the orientation of actions and processes toward the achievement of undebatable ends and aims.

But, says Habermas, things are, unfortunately, not so simple. He distinguishes, in fact, between three separate phases of human history. Very early on in this history the two ways of understanding the world, i.e. communicative and instrumental reason, were still tightly interwoven with one another. Thus in early tribal societies, for example, it was generally the tribal "elders" that decided the sowing, harvesting and hunting times for the whole tribe, when a nomadic tribe would break camp and so on. In other words, the years of experience acquired by these elders over the course of many summers and winters was seen to be so valuable that even "strategic", goal-oriented decisions were made "communicatively", through the deliberations of these experienced men and women.

With the development of technology, however, we begin to see an uncoupling of instrumental reason from communicative reason. Throughout the early centuries of the modern era, with the Reformation and the founding shortly afterward of centralized nation-states and their structures of state administration, there occurs a separation of the two spheres of human experience that Habermas calls respectively "lifeworld" and "system". The "system" begins to become a world of its own, a world of processes and operations steered by power and money that is no longer subject to supervision or control by the communicative decisions and agreements of the interhuman "lifeworld".

Finally there sets in, around the time of the Industrial Revolution, yet a third stage. By now, instrumental thinking has become so powerful that it begins to try to "colonize" the lifeworld and its essentially communicative thinking. In our advanced stage of modernity there is no need or demand for any such thing as a "council of elders". Indeed, on the contrary, any advice offered by older members of society on the basis of their personally acquired knowledge will tend to be seen as "getting in the way". The place of the collective communicative reflection engaged in in the past is taken, now, by the imperative of constant progress, ever more revolutionary inventions, and ever shorter knowledge-innovation cycles. Thus, the economy and other material systems slip ever farther out of control and supervision by the life-world. Indeed, the control tends now to go the other way. This is a phenomenon for which Habermas has coined the term "colonization of the lifeworld":

Today, those imperatives characteristic of the spheres of economy and administration, which are typically governed by the media of money and power, are penetrating into areas of our lives

which are of a nature such that they tend to collapse when they are uncoupled from action aimed at reaching an understanding and switched over, as they are being switched over today, to a governance by money-and power-oriented logics.[43]

Science has also played an important role in this "un-coupling" of the system from the lifeworld. So many key decisions in our societies are no longer taken, through discussion and discourse, by the citizens of these societies but rather by experts, whose reasons for deciding whatever they decide are mostly incomprehensible to the majority of those affected by these decisions. The ever more powerful natural sciences which have brought us, since the Enlightenment, so much technical progress in the fields of medicine, transport and commodity production represent in the end, argues Habermas, a peril for communicative thought and action:

> The empirical-analytical sciences generate technical recommendations [...] The place of emancipation through enlightenment is taken by instruction as to how to gain control over objective, or objectified, processes.[44]

Once again, Habermas's abstract philosophical language may seem a little dismaying. But he is really saying simply this: our daily life tends, today, to be less and less about critically examining the recommendations given by our scientists and engineers and more and more about just following instructions regarding how we are to "function most efficiently" in society. New technical inventions are not discussed but just automatically accepted and applied. Habermas issues a grave warning about this ever blinder "faith in science" displayed by our societies. To the danger that threatens us here he gives the name "scientism":

'Scientism' means science's belief in itself; that is, the conviction that we can no longer understand science as one form of possible knowledge but rather must identify knowledge with science.[45]

"Science" and "knowledge", in other words, are increasingly taken to be one and the same thing. This expresses itself already in the language we hear every day. We have all heard people introduce whatever they are going to say with the phrase: "Studies have shown..." Such phrases mislead us into overlooking the fact that the studies referred to are often studies commissioned by private companies working in the areas, such as food- or drug-production, concerned, so that we must suspect that the results will be skewed toward these companies' interests. And even if the studies in question can claim to be objective and independent of any influence from industry, all scientific knowledge of any sort, Habermas warns us, ought to be critically examined and discussed with a view to its possible longer-term consequences.

When, for example, it first became technically possible to generate energy from atomic power, little or no public discussion was conducted, anywhere in the world, about the opportunities and also the risks created by this new energy source. It was only when the disposal of radioactive waste began to become a problem and when catastrophes in Chernobyl and Fukushima began to shake authorities' faith in the controllability of atomic energy that it became clear that the euphoric speed with which this form of energy-generation had been introduced, using the rationale "we must because we can", had been a serious error. The same applies in many other fields. Be it facial recognition, cosmetic surgery, pre-natal diagnostics or genetically-manipulated foodstuffs, every new scientific theory tends to press for practical application at the very first moment that this seems technically possible:

The socially effective theory is no longer tied to the consciousnesses of human beings who are living and speaking with one another but now rather to the behaviour of human beings tugging and pulling at objective Nature. This theory has altered, indeed, as a powerful new productive force for industrial development, the basis of human life. But it no longer reaches out critically beyond this basis [...].[46]

Habermas issues an urgent warning, then, against trusting to instrumental reason alone and allowing the inventions of our technological age to penetrate, as supposed unquestioned "blessings", deep into our communicative lifeworld:

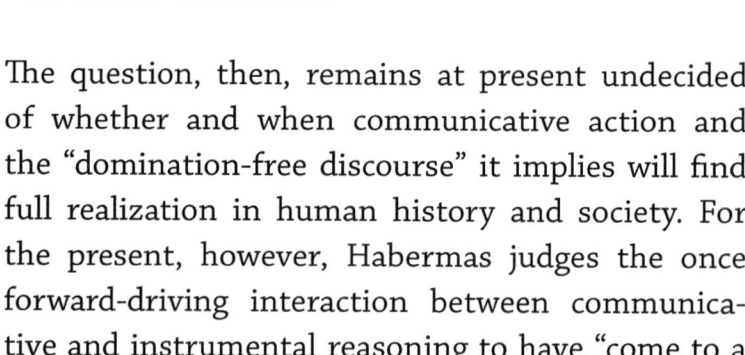

Were this to occur, no rational consensus among citizens about the practical possibility of guiding human history would any longer even be aimed at.

Instead, the aim would become that of attempting to make history something administrable through a perfected technical administration of society.[47]

The question, then, remains at present undecided of whether and when communicative action and the "domination-free discourse" it implies will find full realization in human history and society. For the present, however, Habermas judges the once forward-driving interaction between communicative and instrumental reasoning to have "come to a standstill [...] like a tangled mobile."[48]

Of What Use Is Habermas's Discovery for Us Today?

The Struggle Against the Colonization of the Lifeworld

There can be no doubt but that Habermas has recognized in his philosophical work a key problem afflicting modern society. There is indeed, in today's capitalist world, hardly a single area of life that is not, either directly or indirectly, "governed by the media of money and power".

It is becoming more and more difficult to separate professional life and private life, system and lifeworld. Money and other forms of systemic power really have become like "colonial masters", to use Habermas's striking metaphor, inasmuch as these instrumental, strategic logics have come to govern the actions of human beings and thus to penetrate and conquer larger and larger swathes of the lifeworld, despite this latter being, as we have seen Habermas point out, a sphere

> [...] Of a nature such that it tends to collapse when it is uncoupled from action aimed at reaching an understanding.[49]

One might cite any number of real-life confirmations of Habermas's analysis here. One that springs immediately to my own mind concerns the professional career of a close acquaintance of mine. This young woman made a living selling insurance. Like most people in this line of business she had no fixed sales office of her own but rather visited potential clients at home and made her sales pitches there. I had bought an insurance policy from her myself, since she was a friend of my sister's and I had met her socially. She asked me to recommend her to other potential customers, a request I willingly complied with, since I liked the woman and found, moreover, so far as I could judge such matters, the insurance policy she had sold me to be a good and reasonably-priced one. Through my recommendation, then, another female friend of mine and a male work colleague both ended up buying insurance policies from her.

At a certain point, however, I noticed that I never saw this young woman any more at any of the parties or dinners that my sister liked to arrange for friends and relatives. On asking about her I was told that my sister and all her friends had stopped inviting her because, so they said, "all she ever talks about is how much we need insurance". A while later, I bumped into her by chance on the street and gingerly broached this topic with her. In a resentful tone she complained that it was "a very mean thing to punish her for the way she made her living". "Selling insurance is a face-to-face business," she continued. "People will only buy insurance from someone they know and trust. And trust only develops when friends I've already sold insurance to speak to other friends about the product and tell them it's good and so on. Can't people like your sister see that I depend on her and on people I meet through her for my bread and butter?"

She certainly wasn't wrong about the facts. She depended for her living on the commissions that she got for each new client and the only way she could get new clients was through existing ones, whom she would constantly urge and press to recommend her to friends and friends of friends. But this meant that her material livelihood had, in Habermas's striking phrase, gradually "colonized" her private life. It had commandeered her circle of friends in the service of its own "strategic rationality" of maximizing client-base and resulting profits. What Habermas calls "the governing media of money and power" had, in her life, refused to recognize even communicative, social occasions like parties and private dinners as sacrosanct. All her personal, one-to-one encounters became, as it were, "sales meetings" at which she felt compelled to try to place her product:

[...] The penetration (into the lifeworld) of forms of economic and administrative rationality [...] leads to [...] the objectification of everyday communicative practice.[50]

This "objectification of everyday communicative practice" reached a grotesque extreme when she was informed, in the course of a training seminar run by the big insurance company whose products she made her living placing, that her best chance of making even more sales was to "work on her appearance and her personal charm". The trainers on this course recommended that, since she was a good-looking woman, it would likely be to her advantage to wear short skirts or other slightly revealing outfits during her meetings with potential clients. Surprisingly, or perhaps rather sadly unsurprisingly, her taking this advice did indeed lead to an increase in her sales, at least among male clients. One may say, then, that she ended up assimilating to the "system" of strategic economic thinking to such an extent that she eventually placed not just her private life but even her own body, or at least her bodily appearance, in this "system"'s service:

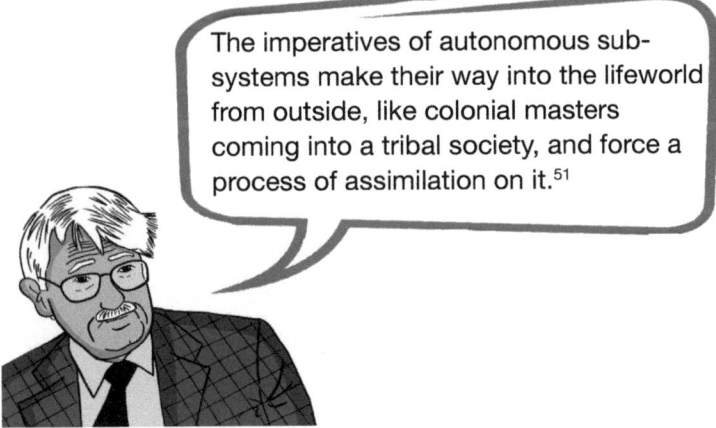

The imperatives of autonomous subsystems make their way into the lifeworld from outside, like colonial masters coming into a tribal society, and force a process of assimilation on it.[51]

In the end, experiences like these led to her giving up this way of making a living altogether. The last straw for her was the large insurance broker's announcement that it would, henceforth, demand that commission earned on sold insurance policies be paid back if the client who had bought a policy cancelled it again after a short period of one, two or three years. This meant, for my acquaintance, constant financial insecurity. Where such repayments of commissions were demanded, her bank account was threatened with slipping, at any time, deep into the red. The large broker told her, indeed, that she could avoid such repayments by re-contacting clients she had sold policies to and persuading them to remain clients after all. But this meant that she would have to devote herself even during holiday periods to constant phone calls to clients she had not seen for years, so she decided just to withdraw from the business and, as she put it, "I'm just glad I'm out of it at last".

This example, as I have said, is just one of hundreds that might be cited of how capitalism, through its sub-systems of money and power, "colonizes" our lifeworld of human contact and communication. Cases exactly similar to the one just cited may, indeed, be becoming rarer, since more and more people now seek insurance online and this particular "face-to-face" business may soon be obsolete anyway. But the "colonization of the lifeworld by the system" is visible in many other areas besides. The rise in "home-office" working and in the free choice of working hours is also proving a fertile ground for such "colonization". Although these new ways of working may appear to offer freedom, earning one's living no longer in terms of measured hours worked but rather in terms of "tasks handled" can often mean that people work much harder at home, while bearing all the overheads themselves, than they would have worked in an office environment with fixed starting and finishing times. Such "home-workers" often also find themselves tacitly accepting that they must be available to customers by telephone at every hour of the day or night. There can also certainly be said to be an ongoing "colonization" of the space of private households by the consumer goods industry. More and more families, above all through the channel of their youngest members, are subject to a kind of compulsion to purchase the latest cell phone or the latest style and brand of trainers.

But above all, perhaps, capitalism shakes and destabilizes our lifeworld through the fear of losing our jobs and of having to live in poverty in our old age. Here Habermas rightly argues the need for a resistance of the lifeworld against its own colonization, for example through people's self-organization in trades unions and other forms of social solidarity:

[...] The socially integrative force of solidarity ought to be able to assert itself effectively against the more violent forces represented by those other means by which our society is guided and moulded: namely, money and administrative power.[52]

Eugenics, the "Self-Optimization" of Humanity: Act Communicatively, Not Instrumentally!

Despite our lifeworld's being visibly "colonized" by instrumental reason in so many different ways, we still find numerous examples of the stubborn persistence in human society of communicative reason and communicative action. This persistence can express itself, as we have just noted, in the form of actions of protest and solidarity. And Habermas himself, indeed, like his near-contemporary, the French philosopher Sartre, has taken an active part, in the course of his long life, in many such actions. Already during his days as a young philosophy assistant at the University of Frankfurt, he made a speech at the great 1958 demonstration against the nuclear rearmament of the army of the German Federal Republic and published an article entitled "Disobedience as the First Among the Duties of the Citizen".

Habermas has also taken a public political stance on the even more controversial issue of eugenics, and one that likely has important consequences for humanity's future. Eugenics too is a topic regarding which communicative reason and instrumental reason tend to directly collide with one another. It is immediately clear what advantage there is in eugenic selection considered from a purely instrumental point of view. Through the analysis of the genetic material present in a fertilized ovum or in the foetus developing from it one can recognize diseases that might manifest themselves later and can choose, by abortion of the foetus or by selection of some other ovum for fertilization, to avoid all the pain and sorrow caused by such diseases.

It is easy, however, to overlook the consequences that can follow from this deciphering of the genetic code as regards the topic we have discussed above: the colonization of the lifeworld by instrumental ac-

tion. In many countries we see how this new technical possibility of prenatal diagnostics is already being
used to create a "child made to order". Such practices,
it is true, still often border on being illegal. But this
does not prevent certain prospective parents from
seeking out, with the help of "friendly" doctors, that
single ovum among many which is apt to produce,
say, a male child with a specific preferred hair- and
eye-colour.

Many argue that such prenatal diagnosis can be, in
certain cases, advantageous. It has long been possible for prospective parents of more advanced age to
find out, by intra-uterine examination, whether the
foetus growing in the womb is likely to develop into
a child suffering from Downs Syndrome, an eventu-
ality which may make for a very difficult future both
for parents and for child, if the pregnancy is brought
to term. Legislatures in many countries have already
recognized that the detection of the genetic disorder
causing Downs Syndrome, called Trisomy 21, is suf-
ficient grounds for proceeding to termination of a
pregnancy.

The progress of science, however, has meant that
many other traits and features of a child can now be
known with certainty many months before its actual
birth. There can no longer be any doubt that the deci-

phering of the genome and the possibility of prenatal diagnostics represent great steps forward for science and might well, in the near future, lead to the effective prevention of all forms of hereditary disease and thus to the emergence of a new, genetically healthy and beautiful form of humanity. Considered from a purely instrumental viewpoint, this is certainly an enticing prospect.

But Habermas raises here two important questions. Firstly, what is currently, and in the near future, instrumentally possible? And secondly, what is actually desirable from the viewpoint of the diversity, naturality and autonomy of our human existence? In other words, the problem he exposes here is the profound and difficult one of the proper limits of Man's power to manipulate his own being.

How much liberty should a democratic society accord to parents, doctors or the state in this matter of the prenatal selection of the characteristics of offspring and where are we obliged to set limits to this liberty? And who exactly is it that should set, in the name of society as a whole, such limits: the Ministry of Health, the President, or some small group of competent scientific experts? In Habermas's view, certainly not the latter, since one thing above all must be avoided:

[...] An elitist splitting-off of expert cultures from contexts of communicative action in daily life.[53]

New genetic dispositions are presently being discovered and deciphered almost daily, which means that there can be predicted with ever greater precision just what kind of disorders, illnesses or even simply what kind of individual traits and characteristics a given child is likely to develop, and at just what point. Our knowledge of our own biological-genetic futures is growing at an incredible rate. But the question is: how are we to handle this knowledge?

Do parents have the right to know at the beginning of a pregnancy, or in the case of artificial insemination even before its beginning, every single trait and detail of their child-to-be, including sex, hair- and eye-colour, anatomy, approximate bodily dimensions etc.? And if the law permits, through regulations issued to doctors, a selection only of certain among these traits and parents are allowed to choose only certain hereditary factors, what kind of choice can, and may, one leave to these parents in the case of multiple fertilized ovula? "Children made to order" have, indeed, now become entirely medically possible. But at what point does there set in a right of the foetus to "be itself"? What moral or legal status is enjoyed by embryos?

In his book *The Future of Human Nature* Habermas urges that the law should forbid what he calls "positive eugenics". By this he means that the law should indeed prevent prospective parents from seeking out and selecting, prenatally, certain physical traits and characteristics of their child-to-be. Every child, argues Habermas, must have the chance to develop, as a youth or even still as an adult, in ways unrestricted by "prior specifications" set by parents and to free him- or herself from all that they may have received in the way of socialization, so as to set out on their own self-determined path. But where "positive eugenics" is permitted, this chance does not exist:

Someone who is at odds with genetically fixed intentions is barred from developing.[54]

Any active or "positive" selection of the traits and characteristics of a child-to-be means, then, an extension of "paternalism" over a free human being that goes far beyond the morally permissible. This is so because parents, in such a case, are determining what natural equipment a future human being is or is not to have without being able to acquire, before doing so, this human being's consent thereto. This same logic that forbids all such "positive eugenics", however, permits, so Habermas argues, the "negative eugenics" of parents' taking preventive prenatal measures to ensure that any child born to them will be free of future serious illnesses. Because in such cases it may reasonably be assumed that the unborn human being *would* give his or her consent to such measures, were they in a position to give consent at all:

Only in the negative case of the prevention of extreme and highly generalized evils may we have good reason to assume that the person concerned would consent to the eugenic goal.[55]

With this idea of a legal prevention only of positive, not of negative, eugenics Habermas has merely made an initial proposal for how to proceed in this area. Most of its questions, however, remain open. What, for example, would actually count here as an "extreme and highly generalized evil" that doctors and parents would be well within their rights in taking measures to prevent? And what would have to count rather as one of the normal risks of human life which must be taken as part of "the rough with the smooth"? Not all those genetic dispositions to illness that are detected do in fact result in illness. Is, then, a mere possibility of falling seriously ill a valid reason to prevent a life's beginning at all?

Indeed, there must in the end also be answered the further question of what age, if any, is an appropriate age to inform a growing young person about the hard genetic facts concerning his or her own person. When can we consider a young person mature enough to deal with the risks and dispositions inherent in his or her genetic code and with the knowledge of their own likely life expectancy?

If Habermas has something important to contribute to debates about these questions then it is surely, even more than the general warning he issues against "positive eugenics", his urging of us never simply to leave the responses to these problems "in the hands of the experts". At the present point in history, he argues, one thing is absolutely crucial: we must not entrust to small elite circles of scientists and scholars the sole power of decision about what direction humanity as a whole is to move in on these questions which so profoundly affect our future. Rather, a broad social discourse and discussion must be conducted on these vital questions and some equally broad consensus be arrived at regarding just which genetic dispositions should preclude a human being's being born into this world and which should not.

The new eugenic possibilities represent a huge challenge for mankind. For hundreds of thousands of years evolution was a process which occurred naturally and entirely outside of Man's control. But the possibility, finally becoming real today, of freeing future human generations from hereditary diseases and even from dispositions to such diseases , or in other words of human biological self-optimization by a kind of "self-breeding", raises some extremely difficult ethical problems which need to be communicatively, not merely technically, solved. There are certainly no quick and easy answers here. The possibilities of mankind's self-optimization through "self-breeding", and the limits that need consciously to be set to these possibilities, will surely be a matter of constant preoccupation not just for this present but for many following generations. But one thing at least is sure: the debate has now begun.

The Third Millennium: A New Barbarism or the Development of Communicative Rationality?

Of what use is Habermas's key idea to us today? Is he right in arguing as he does? Is the entire course of human history indeed characterized by the development of communicative reason in its competition with instrumental reason? And, most importantly, will it in the end be communicative reason which will emerge as predominant all over our world? Will we indeed eventually attain a state of "undamaged and uncompromised intersubjectivity" or will the greater and greater encroachments of instrumental reason lead us into a new barbarism of unrestrained economic exploitation?

Despite his repeated warnings about the colonization of the lifeworld, Habermas is in fact, in the last analysis, rather optimistic regarding these key questions. Because, as we have seen, he is deeply convinced of the fact that a certain emancipatory force is inherent in language itself which must necessarily, in the end, result in agreement through communication and in the realization of the ideal of Reason in communicative form:

> In the validity-claims by which we are obliged, however implicitly, to orient ourselves when we act communicatively there inheres a stubborn, even if constantly suppressed, claim to rationality.[56]

And this "stubborn claim to rationality" will, Habermas firmly believes, continue to exert its effects throughout the course of human history and to leave its mark on social evolution. In his book *Between Facts and Norms: Contributions to a Discourse Theory of Law and Democracy* Habermas shows how communicative reason has gradually given rise to the law and the norms of our democratic societies. Whereas in ancient tribal societies notions of law and social norms tended to be drawn from certain mythological or cosmological ideas or from existing clan- and family-based relations of acknowledged authority, there has emerged more and more in the course of social evolution a generally binding consensus that such laws and norms need in every case to find their legitimation through some form of general discussion or debate. Today, laws can no longer simply be decreed into existence by chieftains, princes or kings with no other justification beyond these figures' "divine right" to do so. Rather, all binding laws require, in some form or another, an intersubjective acknowledgment from the citizens of the state to which they apply. Modern laws are subjected to the test of discourse and discussion by elected parliamentarians and passed by these latter only in their capacities as mandated representatives of the citizens. Ideally, then, the citizens in question should have the sense of being themselves "authors" of these laws:

Citizens must at the same time understand themselves as authors of the law to which they are subject as addressees.[57]

This development leading from traditions, rites and taboos anchored in mythology up to laws and social norms constantly subject to examination and testing by discourse and discussion represents, without any doubt, a form of progress. This progress rests upon an unleashing of communicative reason:

> Through communicative action the rationality potential of language is [...] unleashed [...] in the course of social evolution.[58]

But if this is the case and we do indeed see an "unleashing" of "the rational potentiality of language", or language's "stubborn claim to rationality", in the course of human social evolution then the question naturally arises: how is it that there are still wars? Why has communicative rationality, two thousand years after the beginning of the Christian era and a million years after the emergence of something like human beings on the planet, not yet succeeded in fully developing this supposedly consensus-creating inherent force?

In the end, one must pose to Habermas the same

question as one is obliged to pose to such classical philosophers of history as Hegel or Marx: is there in fact any visible proof of progress in human history? Habermas responds to this question in a way that is unusually personal for a philosopher otherwise known for his extremely scholarly, objective way of proceeding. He confesses both to his readers and to himself that he is "ambivalent" in his attitude to this question. On the one he sees, to his great consternation, that "something has gone deeply wrong" with our rational society. He admits, in other words, that it is definitely not yet the case that communicative reason pervades and guides the social processes that form our lives. On the other hand, however, he is absolutely convinced that communicative rationality has the potential to unfold itself in human history and in fact surely will, at some point, do so:

> There is really nothing to which my attitude is entirely unambivalent – or at least I can claim to feel unambivalently about only very, very few things [...] I am certainly ambivalent inasmuch as I feel that something has indeed gone deeply

wrong with the supposedly rational society in which I grew up and now live. On the other hand, however, I have also retained something of that experience

that all Germans went through in 1945 and since: namely, that from the very bad there has been a move toward the somewhat better. Things really have gotten better. This is a truth on which one must take one's stand.[59]

But is this truth on which Habermas urges us to "take our stand", that "things have gotten somewhat better", really true? Certainly, when one considers the huge interval of time that has elapsed between the ancient world, through the Middle Ages, to the present day it is difficult to disagree with this "truth" of Habermas's. For example, whereas in antiquity slavery was almost universal, with even Aristotle looking on it as something natural, this odious institution has since been abolished in almost every region of the earth.

Considered from this point of view, then, things

surely have "gotten somewhat better". Indeed, this is so even if one narrows the interval examined to comprise just that period since the Second World War that Habermas alludes to when he speaks of "the experience of 1945 and since". Nationalism and Fascism appear to have been overcome; chastened by two world wars, the modern democracies of Europe have joined together in a political and economic union which has succeeded, for the first time in history, in maintaining peace over much of the continent for a period of seventy years. Even the military superpowers, Russia and the USA, have behaved more diplomatically with one another since the end of the Cold War.

It must be said, however, that when one considers certain other social and economic developments of the past few decades, doubts necessarily arise about Habermas's optimistic judgment. In all Western countries we have seen a massive growth in the gap between rich and poor. Large sections of the population feel excluded from the progress and prosperity of society. And precisely that with which Habermas is most concerned, a general participation of all citizens in discussion about social and economic development, is not at all ensured.

On the contrary, many people feel that the purportedly democratic political parties of our societies fail to understand or represent them and have even abandoned them. The increasing number of billionaires on the one hand and people living in abject poverty on the other is driving more and more people into protest movements.

The redistribution of wealth once promised by the "social market economy" appears to have been swept away by a triumphant neo-liberalism. Of what use, then, is Habermas's discovery to us today? Can communicative rationality save us?

As we have seen, Habermas remains in the end ambivalent about this question. One thing, however, he emphasizes again and again: the development of communicative reason, or communicative rationality, is not just some ideal in our heads:

The concept of communicative rationality carries with it connotations based ultimately on the central experience of the unconstrained, unifying, consensus-bringing force of argumentative speech [...].[60]

Communicative rationality, then, is to be traced back to a "central experience" which we can all have.

Dare to Engage in Domination-Free Discourse!

Even though Habermas states that the wish for agreement, and thus the development of freedom and autonomy, is something that inheres in language as a "species-competence", this does not mean that this development is a natural, automatic process and that we need only to stand back and observe how our world gradually becomes an entirely rational one. No. We need at the very least to lend support to the development of the "validity-claims" inherent in speech. Further colonization of the lifeworld can only be prevented if lifeworld discourse, in its turn, attempts to penetrate and pervade the functional systems of power, economy and money:

The systemic spell cast by the capitalist labour market over the life-histories of those able to work

[…] cannot be broken by systems learning to function better. Rather, impulses from the lifeworld must be able to enter into the self-steering of functional systems.[61]

But what specifically does this mean? How can impulses from the lifeworld enter into the functional systems of power and money? How can we possibly communicatively permeate and supervise the economy, i.e. global capitalism? Does humanity still have a chance of surviving? Habermas believes that it has. But the only path forward for the human race is the path of communication:

If we assume that the human species maintains itself through the socially coordinated activities

> and that this coordination is established through communication [...] aimed at reaching agreement [...] then the reproduction of the species also requires satisfying the conditions of a rationality inherent in communicative action.[62]

By "satisfying the conditions of a rationality inherent in communicative action" Habermas means nothing other than the satisfying, so far as possible, of the four validity-claims and the four conditions of the "ideal speech situation". In the end, what he is urging is something very simple: we should, and must, dare to engage in domination-free discourse and not just "ideally" but here and now, in our dealings with our children, friends, neighbours and work colleagues. And this means, at least as a first step, trusting to the "unforced force of the better argument".

It means refusing, wherever possible, all hierarchy and authoritarian tutelage and placing one's hopes rather in agreement achieved through communication. In one's everyday dealings with children it is, of course, a difficult and strenuous thing to provide arguments for one's actions and to achieve, with the very young, an agreement based on discussion. When a very small child is grabbing bars of chocolate off the supermarket shelves and eating them while its mother is seeing to more essential purchases, it will inevitably rather be the "pleasure principle" than "the unforced force of the better argument" that will, with the child, prevail.

In the great majority even of such situations, however, it does make sense to carefully explain to children what is allowed and what is forbidden in our society and to try to establish some "consensus" between them and ourselves. The sooner we succeed in bringing them to actually articulate and argue for their desires and begin to practice together with them a "domination-free discourse", the sooner they will begin to share in responsibility for the society they are growing into and develop a critical sense and awareness of the reality of norms and conventions.

By becoming accustomed, from their earliest years onward, to offering actual reasons and arguments for all the wishes, large and small, that they express and to adjusting and coordinating their needs with those of others, there will also gradually become clear to them the fundamental fact that all rules and procedures of any society are founded in the last analysis in agreements and that these agreements must constantly be examined and, where necessary, revised in light of the cogency of the arguments they are based on. Thus young people learn to give grounds for their claims and compare these grounds with the grounds for other, competing ones:

[...] The rationality of those who participate in this communicative practice is determined by whether they could [...] provide reasons for their expressions.[63]

Rationality, or reason, then, will, argues Habermas develop and flourish everywhere where validity-claims are supported by argument and measured, through discourse, against the validity-claims of others. If human beings have learned anything from the demands of the Enlightenment and the French Revolution and from the experiences of fascism and dictatorship then it is perhaps that veneration of authority and blind obedience to those in power tend to have fatal consequences. With his idea of a "domination-free discourse" Habermas has provided us with a procedure by which we can come to decisions beyond all hierarchy and fixed authority and act in concert and in solidarity.

It is not only within the family but more and more also within the world of work that we are opting to follow the path of discursively-generated decisions and actions. The "teamwork" that is spoken about so much these days has in many companies already become the established corporate culture. Obviously, we cannot really speak of a "domination-free discourse" existing within commercial companies. Indeed, even the just-mentioned "teamwork" is often not at all what it appears to be. The boss will often, after having allowed his "team" to discuss and argue for a time about what needs to be done, still take, as in "the old days", the final decision by himself alone.

For example, in one globally leading insurance group an expensive initiative was mounted by the Human Resources department under the motto "management from equal to equal". The initiative was well-intentioned, progressive and sounded, indeed, like an attempt to implement something like Habermas's "domination-free discourse". It was foreseen that the employees should be able to talk, as equals to equals, with the company boss about the best strategy for the group and the best decisions to be taken. In this way, it was hoped, the creativity and potential of each individual employee as a provider of new ideas and an initiator of action could be drawn into the whole corporate process and everyone could be motivated to take part responsibly in decision-making. The Human Resources department asked all the other departments for feedback on this new corporate culture as it was introduced.

The practical result of all this, however, was only that each of the top-level managers called all of the department sub-managers in to a meeting and asked them, one by one, whether they had the feeling that they were being allowed freely and unrestrictedly to contribute their ideas, plans and proposals. Naturally, for fear of saying the wrong thing, each manager repeated the "safe" answer that everything was going just as hoped and that the "teamwork" plan was working out fine. Once this same ritual of confirmation had been run through between the sub-managers and the still lower managers subordinate to them and between these latter and the simple employees, the Human Resources department received, of course, in the end, the satisfying feedback that "management from equal to equal" had indeed been successfully implemented throughout the group.

Just this self-deluding upshot, both comical and sad at once, of a well-intentioned project like "management from equal to equal" points up very clearly how there were in fact lacking here the necessary preconditions for a "domination-free discourse". Indeed, the very notion of such an initiative must be said to contain, from Habermas's point of view, a certain internal contradiction, since in Habermas's "ideal speech situation" every participant must enjoy an equal authority right from the start if the situation is really to be discursively "ideal", so that the notion of a "manager" cannot, here, really apply. Furthermore, the practice itself of asking the employees for their views on the initiative was inadequate, from the very start, from a discourse-ethical viewpoint, since the asking itself did not occur within a "domination-free" discursive environment. Nevertheless, the initiative represented a start, a first tentative effort to soften and loosen up, in one of the biggest insurance companies in the world, the hierarchical structures of communication.

But this example shows us how long a way we have still to go until we can actually create a "domination-free discourse" in the business world. This "ideal speech-situation" is also the main point of critical attack for those who reject Habermas's key ideas. Because, so Habermas's critics argue, the notion of "domination-free discourse" necessarily presupposes the existence of an "ideal speech-situation" and no such situation can in fact ever exist. In reality, decisions cannot be talked through in an environment free of all authority either in the family or in a commercial company or in political life. In none of these environments do the discussing parties enjoy that equal private or professional authority that would alone allow them to follow just the "forceless force of the better argument" and thus to arrive at a consensus. Nor in any of these real situations will the participants be such that they articulate their contributions on the basis of equal social origin, education, life-experience and discursive talent.

For example, in a conversation within the family the father and mother will tend to enjoy, just by reason of their longer life-experience, more authority than the growing children. The owner of a business will have more economic power, more commercial know-how, and perhaps indeed even more genuine concern for the welfare of the company than someone who is merely an employee of this latter. A Prime Minister will have more power than the members of his cabinet. A general will have greater power of decision than his officers. And a professor will have more authority than his students. Such a thing as a truly "domination-free discourse", we may say, in which all participants discuss on a truly "even playing field", is to be found only among good friends chatting over a glass of beer or in a conversation between man and wife – and even there consensus can often not be arrived at.

Habermas's model also involves the risk of an "endless discussion" developing, namely in the case where the participants prove unable to agree through a process of argument and cannot reduce their respective needs to some common denominator. Habermas's "discourse ethics", then, his critics argue, is in the end impracticable and just a form of idealism after all. There is no "ideal speech situation" in actual lived reality. Nor would it ever be possible, by making the counter-factual assumption that such an "ideal speech situation" should be treated hypothetically as existing, to achieve in this way some discursive agreement. It is also often objected that Habermas's writings on discourse ethics, numerous and extensive though they are, in fact end up providing no substantive guidelines for action. This, indeed, is something that Habermas himself concedes:

> To that extent discourse ethics can properly be characterized as *formal*, for it provides no substantive guidelines but only a procedure: practical discourse.[64]

Despite this threefold critique levelled against it, however, one should definitely not underestimate the key idea at the core of Habermas's philosophy. It is true, indeed, that discourse ethics is really only a formal procedure. Likewise, it is true that an "ideal speech situation" is never, or only extremely seldom, to be encountered in real life. And finally, it is also true that it is extremely difficult and time-consuming to find ways of drawing all individual needs and arguments into the process of finding a consensus.

Nonetheless, with his demand for a "domination-free discourse" Habermas has brought something into the world which will likely henceforth always play a role in human culture. Perhaps decades will have to pass before we are in a position to realize the notion of "domination-free discourse" in all the relevant social spheres and thereby to fill this notion with life. Perhaps even centuries, if we are to suppose that, as Habermas intends, the entire world can and must develop its potential for discursive decision and action. But even if we never succeed in realizing, worldwide, "domination-free discourse" in its pure form, it remains the case that the path pointed out by Habermas has a "revolutionarily" emancipatory goal.

In the last analysis, we may say that Habermas has thought through, in a new and radical way, the demands raised by the French Revolution for "liberty, equality and fraternity" and has provided us, through his "discourse ethics", with a procedure for implementing these and putting them into practice. Because in "domination-free discourse" we can all "equally" articulate our specific needs and arguments, exchange our different views "fraternally", and agree "freely" on a common course of action. In other words, it is only discursively that the ideals of "liberty, equality and fraternity" can, in the end, be realized.

What is more, Habermas has given an example for this is in his own life. He has been, as a scholar, involved in many bitter polemics and has both received and dished out many often damning critiques. But it must be conceded to him that he trusted, in every case, to "the forceless force of the better argument". He has revised his position, in the light of others' critiques, several times and has indeed, more than perhaps any other philosopher before him, drawn the arguments and philosophies of other thinkers into his own.

There can be no question, then, of dismissing "domination-free discourse" as just a theoretical construct and "pure idealism". It is certainly a living thing. We sense its reality most keenly, perhaps, when it is refused us and we feel that we are being discursively ignored. Because everywhere where "the forceless force of the better argument" yields to power, where we are not understood or not even listened to, we feel a sense of oppression and wrong. And conversely, where something like this "domination-free discourse" actually takes place, or at least the attempt is made to let it take place, it will never fail to give rise to the feeling of a successfully achieved, intact and undamaged intersubjectivity of the sort that has remained the guiding light for Habermas throughout his philosophical career:

There is, inarguably, a certain intellectual motif and basic intuition that has always guided my work. [...] This intuition [...] aims at the experience of an undamaged intersubjectivity,

something more fragile than anything that the history of the structures of human communication has hitherto brought forth from itself.[65]

Bibliographical References

1   Habermas, On the Logic of the Social Sciences, MIT Press, Cambridge Massachussetts, 1988, p. 117.

2   Habermas, Knowledge and Human Interests, Beacon Press, Boston, 1971, p. 314

3   Habermas, The Theory of Communicative Action, Volume One, Beacon Press, Boston, 1984, p. 287

4   Habermas, Knowledge and Human Interests, Beacon Press, Boston, 1971, p. 314

5   Habermas, Between Facts and Norms, MIT Press, Cambridge Massachussetts, 1996, p. 306

6   Habermas, Knowledge and Human Interests, Beacon Press, Boston, 1971, p. 314

7   Habermas, On the Pragmatics of Social Interaction, MIT Press, Cambridge Massachussetts, 2001, p. 136

8   Habermas, On the Logic of the Social Sciences, MIT Press, Cambridge Massachussetts, 1988, p. 117.

9   Habermas, Kleine Politische Schriften I-IV, Suhrkamp, Frankfurt, 1981, p. 486.

10 Ibid.

11 Habermas, Knowledge and Human Interests, Beacon Press, Boston, 1971, p. 314.

12 Habermas, On the Pragmatics of Social Interaction, MIT Press, Cambridge Massachussetts, 2001, p. 62

13 Ibid.

14 Ibid. p. 132.

15 Ibid. p. 97-98

16 Habermas, On the Pragmatics of Communication, MIT Press, Cambridge Massachussetts, 1998, p. 22

17 Ibid.

18 Ibid.

19 Ibid.

20 Ibid.

21 Habermas, Knowledge and Human Interests, Beacon Press, Boston, 1971, p. 314

22 Habermas, Dialektik der Rationalisierung, in Juergen Habermas im Gespraech mit Axel Honneth, Aesthetik und Kommunikation, issue 45/46, 1981, p. 151 ff.

23 Habermas, Kleine Politische Schriften I-IV, Suhrkamp, Frankfurt, 1981, p. 486.

24 Habermas, Wahrheitstheorien, in Fahrenbach (ed.) Wirklichkeit und réflexion, Festschrift zum 60ten Geburtstag von Walter Schulz, Pfullingen 1973, p. 255.

25 Ibid. p. 256

26 Ibid. p. 255

27 Ibid. p. 255

28 Ibid. p. 256

29 Ibid. p. 258

30 Ibid.

31 Immanuel Kant, Critique of Practical Reason, in Mary J. Gregor (ed) Kant's Practical Philosophy, Cambridge University Press, 2015, p. 28.

32 Habermas, Moral Consciousness and Communicative Action, Polity Press, Cambridge, 1992, p. 67

33 Ibid.

34 Habermas, The Theory of Communicative Action, Volume One, Beacon Press, Boston, 1984, p. 392.

35 Ibid. p. 391.

36 Ibid.

37 Ibid.

38 Habermas, Knowledge and Human Interests, Beacon Press, Boston, 1971, p. 314.

39 Habermas , Theorie und Praxis, Frankfurt am Main, 1971, p. 350 (not translated into English).

40 Habermas, Theory of Communicative Action, Volume Two, Beacon Press, Boston, 1984, p. 126.

41 Habermas , Technik und Wissenschaft als Ideologie, Frankfurt am Main, 1968, p. 63 (not translated into English).

42 Habermas , Theorie und Praxis, Frankfurt am Main, 1971, p. 16 (not translated into English).

43 Habermas Die Neue Unuebersichtlichkeit , Suhrkamp, Frankfurt, 1985, p. 189 (not translated into English).

44   Habermas , Theorie und Praxis, Frankfurt am Main, 1971, p. 308
     (not translated into English).
45   Habermas, Knowledge and Human Interests, Beacon Press, Boston,
     1971, p. 4.
46   Habermas , Theorie und Praxis, Frankfurt am Main, 1971, p. 308 (not
     translated into English).
47   Ibid. p. 232.
48   Habermas, Moral Consciousness and Communicative Action, Polity
     Press, Cambridge, 1992, p. 19
49   Habermas Die Neue Unuebersichtlichkeit , Suhrkamp, Frankfurt,
     1985, p. 189 (not translated into English).
50   Habermas, Theory of Communicative Action, Volume Two, Beacon
     Press, Boston, 1984, p. 321 (translation altered).
51   Ibid. p. 355.
52   Habermas Die Neue Unuebersichtlichkeit , Suhrkamp, Frankfurt,
     1985, p. 158 (not translated into English).
53   Habermas, The Theory of Communicative Action, Volume Two, Beacon   Press, Boston, 1984, p. 330.
54   Habermas, The Future of Human Nature, Polity Press, Cambridge UK,
     p. 62
55   Ibid. p. 63
56   Habermas, Kleine Politische Schriften I-IV, Suhrkamp, Frankfurt,
     1981, p. 486.
57   Habermas, Between Facts and Norms : Contributions to a Discourse
     Theory of Law and Democracy, MIT Press, Cambridge Massachusetts,
     p. 408
58   Ibid. p. 42.
59   Habermas, Dialektik der Rationalisierung, in Juergen Habermas im
     Gespraech mit Axel Honneth, Aesthetik und Kommunikation, issue
     45/46, 1981, p. 152.
60   Habermas, The Theory of Communicative Action, Volume One,
     Beacon Press, Boston 1984, p. 10
61   Habermas, The Philosophical Discourse of Modernity, MIT Press,
     1987, p. 364.
62   Habermas, The Theory of Communicative Action, Volume One,
     Beacon Press, Boston 1984, p. 397.

63 Ibid. p. 17.

64 Habermas, Moral Consciousness and Communicative Action, MIT Press 1990, p. 103

65 Habermas, Dialektik der Rationalisierung, in Juergen Habermas im Gespraech mit Axel Honneth, Aesthetik und Kommunikation, issue 45/46, 1981, pp. 151-2.

Already published in the same series:

Walther Ziegler
Camus in 60 Minutes
ISBN 9783741227738

Walther Ziegler
Freud in 60 Minutes
ISBN 9783741227707

Walther Ziegler
Hegel in 60 Minutes
ISBN 9783741227677

Walther Ziegler
Heidegger in 60 Minutes
ISBN 9783741227752

Walther Ziegler
Kant in 60 Minutes
ISBN 9783741226373

Walther Ziegler
Marx in 60 Minutes
ISBN 9783741227691

Walther Ziegler
Nietzsche in 60 Minutes
ISBN 9783752803822

Walther Ziegler
Platon in 60 Minutes
ISBN 9783741227615

Walther Ziegler
Sartre in 60 Minutes
ISBN 9783741227653

Walther Ziegler
Rousseau in 60 Minutes
ISBN 9783741227622

Walther Ziegler
Smith in 60 Minutes
ISBN 9783741227721

Walther Ziegler
Rawls in 60 Minutes
ISBN 9783750424050

Walther Ziegler
Wittgenstein in 60 Minutes

Walther Ziegler
Adorno in 60 Minutes

Walther Ziegler
Hobbes in 60 Minutes

Walther Ziegler
Popper in 60 Minutes

Walther Ziegler
Habermas in 60 Minutes

Coming soon in the same series:

Walther Ziegler
Arendt in 60 Minutes

Walther Ziegler
Foucault in 60 Minutes

Walther Ziegler
Schopenhauer in 60 Minutes

Walther Ziegler
Konfuzius in 60 Minutes

The author:

Dr Walther Ziegler is academically trained in the fields of philosophy, history and political science. As a foreign correspondent, reporter and newsroom coordinator for the German TV station ProSieben he has produced films on every continent. His news reports have won several prizes and awards. He has also authored numerous books in the field of philosophy. His many years of experience as a journalist mean that he is able to present the complex ideas of the great philosophers in a way that is both engaging and very clear. Since 2007 he has also been active as a teacher and trainer of young TV journalists in Munich, holding the post of Academic Director at the Media Academy, a University of Applied Sciences that offers film and TV courses at its base directly on the site of the major European film production company Bavaria Film. After the huge success of the book series "Great thinkers in 60 Minutes", he works as a freelance writer and philosopher.